"Defining your values sounds great but can be just as ambiguous as trying to 'find your purpose.' Bradley Hook has written the definitive guide on values—the what, how and why—in a friendly and engaging manner. This book is a must-read for any leader looking to bring greater clarity and meaning to their life."

—Rachel Hamlin, executive coach and mindset expert

"Do you want a more fulfilling and happy life? *Start With Values* by Bradley Hook, is a must read. This easy-to-read book identifies the crucial role that values play in your life. You also learn practical tools to discover and define your core values, turn your values into habits and practice, and build a more meaningful life with satisfying relationships – all backed by research and science."

—Dr. Terri Orbuch, PhD, author of *5 Simple Steps to Take Your Marriage from Good to Great*

PRAISE FOR
START WITH VALUES

"In a world where external pressures often cloud our true desires, Bradley Hook's *Start With Values* serves as a clear guide to authenticity. By leading readers through a simple yet thoughtful process to identify their top three values, he offers a profound yet straightforward approach. His riveting narratives, coupled with scientific insights, highlight the importance of living in alignment with our core values and the principles that ground us. This book is a classic treasure. The process for determining your values is fun, profound and awe-inspiring!"

—Alice Inoue, author, life expert & founder of Happiness U

"I have had the privilege of knowing and working with Bradley Hook for nearly two decades. He has been an inspiration to me both personally and professionally. In his latest body of work, *Start with Values,* Brad provides clear insights and understanding into what I believe is the vital core, guiding rudder, internal compass, and "magic potion" to happiness and success in life: clarity on your values. The secret to life certainly does all Start With Values. I can't recommend this book enough, as it could well be the start of your revitalized life."

—Ian Hutchinson, founder & Chief Engagement
Officer for Life by Design

"*Start With Values* provides a compass that can help you navigate the complexities of modern life. It will help you find your north star, your purpose, as well as yourself. If leading a worthy life matters to you—and I suspect it does—I recommend you start with this book."
—Tal Ben-Shahar, PhD, New York Times
bestselling author of *Happier, No Matter What*

"Brad Hook's book is an engaging, heartwarming and insightful read. It is a powerful wake-up call to the realization that our values are the source of our actions—and a very timely one. Brad provides an actionable pathway to live a fulfilling life through owning and being responsible for our core values."
—Lloyd Fickett, founder of The Collaborative Way®
and co-author of *The Collaborative Way*

"Brad Hook takes you on a light, engaging and integral journey into the role of values in life. Simply and clearly, he guides you through a process to define and focus on those values that really matter to you. Then, and in my view most importantly, he shows you how to link your chosen values into practical, achievable actions that can be built into your day—and then progressively into your life. *Start With Values* is a keeper. You can work your way through all of it or you can dive into the parts that call to you. Go back to it and keep your values alive and aligned."
—Dr. Sven Hansen, MBChB, MBA, founder of
The Resilience Institute

"Defining our values is an essential step to fulfilment...yet few of us take the time to do so. Bradley Hook is the ideal guide to set us on this journey. Your future self will thank you for reading this book."
—David Robson, author of *The Expectation Effect* and
The Laws of Connection

START WITH
VALUES

START WITH VALUES

HOW TO BUILD A LIFE WITH MEANING AND PURPOSE

BRADLEY HOOK

Hatherleigh Press is committed to preserving and protecting the natural resources of the earth. Environmentally responsible and sustainable practices are embraced within the company's mission statement.

Visit us at www.hatherleighpress.com.

START WITH VALUES

Library of Congress Cataloging-in-Publication Data is available upon request.
ISBN: 978-1-961293-10-6

Printed in the United States
10 9 8 7 6 5 4 3 2 1

For those who seek.

CONTENTS

INTRODUCTION

MY EARLIEST MEMORIES are of blistering sun. My pale skin erupting in freckles, desperate to shield me from an environment to which my complexion was not suited. That sun would be my nemesis, turning my skin red and causing an endlessly peeling epidermis throughout my childhood.

However, back then, we didn't worry about the sun's dangers. Life was simple. Eat, drink, move. Play with the dogs. Avoid my mother when she rubbed her face because that meant trouble. Stay out of the way when arguments between her and my stepfather reached boiling point, which they often did. I'll never forget how my mother lay sprawled across the kitchen floor after being violently thrown across the room. She was eight months pregnant, and I was a helpless nine-year-old. Holes accumulated in drywalls and doors as my stepfather's temper flared. Then, without fail, I'd detect what I'd later recognize as the sweet smell of *Durban Poison*—a world-famous strain of cannabis—and they'd emerge from their room smiling and hungry. I was grateful that they found a way to achieve calm, even if it was transient.

As a teenager, I noticed my increasing strength. The sun baked down over dusty rugby fields, where we put our bodies on the line every weekend during winter. The sun burnt my face when I started surfing, a pursuit that changed my life. There's nothing in the world like crouching into a wave's heart space and watching that crystal cylinder unravel as you race from within the tube back towards the light. It's all color, motion, desperation, and delight.

I remember the humidity of Durban in summer. Thunderstorms that arrived like a dark blanket, tugged by westerly winds across the sky. Being whipped with a bamboo stick by middle-aged high school teachers for not doing things I was supposed to do. The long walk to the principal's office, knowing exactly what lay in store. Adrenaline, dry mouth, full-blown activation of flight mode but only one choice: to move forward, to face the music. The principal would run a piece of chalk down his cane so that the line on my trousers from the first strike would provide a target for the second and third. Then there was the exhilaration of walking back out into the blazing sun and realizing I had survived. Around this time, I developed a deep resentment towards people who intentionally hurt others or abused positions of power.

Growing up in South Africa, I was confronted with questions about race and heritage. Why did we never see black children? Why did black people clean houses and schools but not work in offices, hospitals or shops? The black people I met had stories to share—they were no less than we were—yet they were not allowed on our streets at night, and they lived far away in "townships," places we dared not venture.

While high school history lessons spun a narrative about the simultaneous arrival into Southern Africa of white settlers from Europe and African people migrating from the north, my grandfather's tales of ancient cave art, San hunter-gatherer tribes, and African warriors painted a richer forbidden history. I realized early that you should never blindly trust those in power. However, I also realized that most people have good intentions, including those who have supported or been trampled by a system like apartheid.

Lying in bed at my father's house every second weekend, I could sometimes hear machine gun fire and helicopters hovering over some atrocity that I couldn't quite comprehend. The townships were growing, edging closer to white suburbia. But we hid behind security gates and windows with bars, guarded by hypervigilant attack dogs, captives in our own homes, dashing only to the safety of work, school, the mall, and in my case, the beach.

My grandfather was more than just a storyteller; he was my introduction to the world of values. With unwavering generosity—often referred to as his "long pockets"—he demonstrated the values of kindness and service. He made time for everyone, from homeless people to high-level executives from Japan, and me. He was one of the few people who traveled internationally from South Africa during apartheid, because he sourced products from Asia for his employer, a large retail store. He smelt like cigarettes and Old Spice. He wore a beige safari suit beneath smiling eyes. Then he was gone. The cigarettes cut his time short—he was only 62 when cancer overwhelmed his lungs and body. But he said he didn't regret smoking, he'd enjoyed his life and wouldn't change anything, even if given another chance. I wonder if he meant that. I'd love to have spent a bit more time with him, but I sense that he's still here, his values living on through me. Human bodies come and go, but stories and values transcend our fragile physical form.

That's why they are important.

My father was a sports star and a businessman. Calm, tall and gracious, he was my first hero. He never lost his cool, and I thank him for demonstrating how to lead through adversity and motivate through action. Until he reads this, he probably doesn't know how grateful I am to have had his presence amidst the chaos that was my youth. I tried to push him to shout at me, to lash out and prove that the world wasn't a good place, but he always remained calm. Testament to his kind nature, he even progressed up the corporate ladder during the time of Black Economic Empowerment, which was a form of affirmative action to redistribute jobs and wealth. He mentored the next generation of leaders on their own journeys and was both loved and respected for his skill and empathy. As a teenager, I drifted towards misadventure and saw him less and less until it was a couple of times per year.

Sometimes I'd roam the night, walking for miles to go to parties or sneak into bars. The quest for freedom—and oblivion—leads many young people to explore the fringe between safety and danger. I experienced some attempted muggings and encountered people with bad intent, but my worst enemy during those times was myself.

At age 18, I was ejected at high speed through the windscreen of my mother's company car when it veered off a freeway a few hours before dawn. I woke up to discover my best friend trapped in an upside-down wreck, somehow alive. This changed my life. I experienced deep presence throughout the recovery and felt gratitude for my second chance, having been so close to death. There's nothing like finding glass fragments embedded in your scalp several weeks after an accident.

Around that time, my beloved dog—a brindle Staffordshire Bull Terrier, was enticed into the bushes by the vervet monkeys that lived at the end of our garden. He was silly enough to chase them into their territory, never to be seen again.

A few months later, I had a motorcycle accident on my way to the bar where I worked. An oil spill on the road caused me to slide out and crash into a barrier, only a few hundred meters from where the car accident had occurred. After this incident, I spiraled downward fast, escaping reality in the depths of rave clubs, where throbbing music and green lasers gave me something to cling to.

I knew it was time to leave Africa. I felt that I needed a geographic change, and the UK offered a two-year holiday visa to South Africans. My first ever flight landed in London, where, at age 19, I found a job as a private security contractor. I was quickly promoted from prestigious art galleries to high-end office skyscrapers because I was proactive, a good listener and had an excellent memory for detail. Plus, I successfully apprehended someone who threw ink across a priceless work of art.

Although I had enjoyed spending time in places like the Royal Academy of Arts, I was happy to no longer be searching handbags or staring at Damien Hirst exhibits all day. Trust me, after several months of standing beside a glass box art installation, where maggots emerge from a cow's head, turn into flies and get zapped by a fly zapper, you're ready for change.

Speaking to office workers in the building I was guarding, I became curious about opportunities in business. Setting aside my dream of becoming a photojournalist, I knocked up a CV, purchased a cheap suit, and plunged headfirst into the corporate world. By "plunge," I quite literally mean descending into the dingy depths of a filing room, where I spent my days making coffee for my manager, reading literature, writing, and occasionally filing something. Within two years, I was a well-paid business analyst at one of the UK's largest telecommunications companies.

To do this, I leveraged my innate curiosity to master computer programming, automating complex operational processes and saving the company hundreds of thousands of pounds. I valued creativity and found that I could create amazing things using any medium. Back in South Africa, I had studied photography and media, and I was commercially successful, published and paid for my work within months of starting the course. I was a fast learner and, thanks to my mother, honestly believed that anything was possible.

I changed jobs, always taking on more responsibilities, wearing uncomfortable suits and navigating archaic corporations in my own curious way. But cubicle walls began to feel stifling. I drank pints with colleagues at lunch time and did handstands in the bathroom to break up the monotony. Relentless grey clouds hung over old London town. Endless drizzle. I arrived at work in the dark and left when it was darker. I understood why the Beatles sang with joy about the sun returning. For the first time in my life, I longed for it too.

I made many friends in the UK, and shared a house where most of my cohabitants were Australian. Tales of golden beaches and waves eventually led me to Sydney, where the sky seemed bluer and the horizon wider than anywhere I had previously been. I drove across the country in a 1972 VW Kombi, awestruck by the sheer scale of the place. Around every coastal headland was a golden beach with endlessly peeling waves. I surfed my brains out.

After establishing a digital agency, I built digital platforms for many organizations. I had a team of developers in India back in 2001, long before outsourcing became popular. I was always entrepreneurial and loved new ideas. While success seemed relatively natural, challenges were never far behind.

My mother had a double stroke from a brain aneurysm when she was 49. She had emigrated to the UK shortly before I left for Australia. After arriving to visit her in 2005, I was told she had been admitted to hospital. I spent Christmas Eve in a rental car in the hospital car park, wondering if they would turn off life support the next day. The doctor said he would ask for my permission. Curled up and shivering on the back seat, I was reminded of the values my mother instilled in me—particularly her belief in freedom and limitless potential. Ironically, her own freedom was taken away and she was destined to spend the rest of her life as a quadriplegic in a nursing home.

Throughout my twenties, interactions with great thought leaders like Ian Hutchinson and Malcolm McLeod sculpted my understanding of the world. Their teachings on positive psychology, goal setting, well-being and work-life balance were transformative. Their relentless optimism challenged my inner dialogue. I also learned about being an entrepreneur and that caring for your people is the key to business success.

Despite soaking up this inspiration, I ventured down some dark paths. Ruthless extremes, from exhilarating highs in the party scene to debilitating burnouts from my workaholic tendencies, led me to a deep depression. On the surface, I was a happy, carefree guy who loved surfing and socializing, yet beneath the veneer, I was suffering.

But a flicker of hope remained. I knew I could achieve something worthwhile. I invented a carbon offsetting system for digital technology, planting trees to offset web server electricity consumption, but gave up on it due to investor pressure, misaligned values, and my own lack of resilience. I also founded an online surfing magazine, surfd.com, that decades later has become one of the world's leading resources for surfers. Together with Ian Hutchinson, I built world-first employee engagement and well-being platforms that were eventually used by tens of thousands of people at many of Australia's largest companies. Positive psychology, neuroscience, mindfulness and integrative health were areas that sparked immense curiosity. I immersed myself in these fields, unwittingly becoming a keen practitioner—if not yet an expert— in personal empowerment and behavior change.

My reputation for delivering excellent digital experiences enabled me to follow in the footsteps of Tim Ferriss and become a remote-working "digital nomad" in my thirties. It was after a particularly messy break-up that I activated my value of freedom, packed up my life, gave everything away and purchased a one-way ticket to India.

Over the next few years, I achieved my dream of becoming a photojournalist. I created cover stories for magazines, capturing photographs and writing text about places few travelers had been. I pushed the limits, going broke in Bangladesh, surfing the Baltic Sea, learning magic in India and being challenged by Kung Fu masters in Vietnam. I interviewed people who were masters in their fields, always trying to uncover the secrets to sustainable high performance—something I aspired to achieve. Through all of this, I realized something important: most people are good. Most people would like nothing more than to invite you to their home to share a meal.

I cried, much to the concern of a family in Goa, while consuming a dinner of tiny silver fish cooked in spices that blew my mind. Even water from the local well—not recommended for travelers at the best of times—would not soothe the fire in my mouth. I used camera lens tissues to dry my tears and nose, because tissues and toilet paper are not really a thing in these places. If you're interested, I soldiered through three tiny fish while sitting on the only chair in the house, positioned across from an extended family—around 20 people—who sat cross-legged on the floor, watching intently. I'll never forget that family, sharing what little they had with me.

I wrote a book about surfing while suffering from an intestinal parasite in Kathmandu. I climbed the Himalayas with a friend, realizing that the most important part of life is stopping to appreciate the view. Cafes and hotel rooms, internet connections, strangers who became friends and sometimes lovers...we all left our mark on each other.

I remember sitting in a temple with four "babas"—holy men— none of whom could speak English, yet we communicated without words. I lay in a field with a shaman as plant medicine shattered and reassembled my reality like a kintsugi vase. Then I went surfing beneath a cliff in a tiny town in Kerala, gliding along waves on the Arabian Sea. I was in my prime. The sun no longer burned me the way it used to. As an adult, I had grown more resilient, accepting— even welcoming—its stare.

I studied eastern mysticism and philosophy, learning completely new perspectives on health, well-being and the nature of reality. Conversations with monks and spiritual teachers challenged my beliefs and nudged me to adopt a more holistic view of life and time. I attempted to devise unified theories of everything, exploring ideas like infinite loops—the theory that infinity at a cosmic level loops back to infinity at the quantum level. Though still naïve, my value of curiosity was rampantly engaged in the study of who we are, why we're here and what it all means. Teachings by people like Alan Watts and Osho demonstrated that one could both be serious and "an irreducible rascal"—or, as they say in Australia, a larrikin. Perhaps Miyamoto Musashi, the legendary samurai, said it best with, "Think lightly of yourself and deeply of the world."

One day, while studying in an ashram near Mangalore, I wandered through paddy fields flanked by a few lonely palms. My only company was the occasional ibis, standing on one leg, pecking listlessly. I watched the sun cast diamonds upon the dark water, and I felt that my grandfather was there. This sensation has stayed with me ever since.

The journey continued and I met my future partner outside a bar in Bali. She looked like the singer Shakira, or perhaps the goddess Shakti—she was too beautiful to stare at for long. A Russian surfer girl with tanned skin and taught limbs, she was a lioness, and fiercely intoxicating. We reconnected on the island of Tenerife a few months later. Perhaps we had too much fun; soon we were unexpectedly expecting a child. My nomadic adventure, at least for a while, would come to an end.

We moved to New Zealand, where impending parenthood ushered in a new chapter. Shedding the skin of youth was painful, but my values evolved, shifting from freedom and adventure towards patience, kindness, and security.

I met Dr. Sven Hansen from the Resilience Institute and began a life-changing collaboration. Dr. Sven is a genius and I'm deeply grateful for his belief in me, despite the ups and downs of business. For the next decade, I immersed myself in the evidence-based field of human resilience, designing digital platforms, working on research projects, writing books, and delivering workshops to hundreds of companies and tens of thousands of people worldwide. My travels continued, but with a new focus on uplifting others. That's why I'm writing this for you now.

Why core values? Throughout my journey, I have discovered that many high performers feel a lack of purpose, while people with few material possessions can feel deeply fulfilled. Purpose can seem grandiose and unattainable, so I asked myself: what really drives the behaviors of not just humans, but all living creatures? What causes distress when we go astray? Why do some behaviors lead to fulfillment and happiness? The answer lies in our values.

Values guide us, despite the noise and haste of our lives. They determine whether an event is stressful or enriching. Using values to make decisions will give your life direction, allowing you to lean into what is meaningful and right.

Ultimately, I hope that you will experience fulfillment, which happens to be the most important factor supporting the most resilient people. Acting in alignment with your values is like living your own spiritual practice. But remember, it is a practice. That's why I will share a range of tools that close the knowing-doing gap and help you overcome resistance to change. If you want to skip the theory and get straight to the tools, please go directly to the second section of this book.

Are you ready?

1

WHAT ARE VALUES?

DEFINING A VALUE

THE TERM "VALUE" has roots in the Old French *valoir*, meaning "be worth," and derived from the Latin *valere*, meaning "to be strong, be of value." Interestingly, the word "valiant" also traces its roots back to *valere*.

Core values are named as such because they represent what is most important to each of us. Living in alignment with our core values is a valiant act. It requires a clear mind, a calm body, vitality, resilience, and a commitment to stand up for what we believe. Consider a storybook knight—calm and steadfast, even in adversity. Values-aligned action imbues us with that kind of resolve, resilience, and confidence. Confidence is trust in oneself, which stems from knowing what you value. In this light, to "value" something means more than just appreciating its worth; it means making a commitment to protect and cherish what is most important to you.

But what is the difference between values, morals, beliefs, and purpose?

Glad you asked. Values are the things most important to you or your group. Beliefs are convictions or acceptances that certain things are true. Morals are standards of right and wrong, often rooted in specific belief systems. Purpose is the "why" behind our journey in life. (Most of us are not entirely clear about our purpose, but this book will reveal how values-aligned behavior can lead to an emergent sense of purpose.)

Interestingly, people can share a value—such as health—but hold entirely different beliefs about how to be healthy. One person might believe that healthcare and medical intervention secure health, whereas another believes in a healthy lifestyle. Beliefs and values can—and do—change, and they both drive behavior. Starting with values is powerful because by knowing what is most important to us, we can challenge limiting beliefs and reaffirm those that are aligned with our values.

Sometimes our values and behaviors align so naturally that values fade into the backdrop of our lives, unnoticed but ever-present, like a heartbeat. It is often not until a value is violated—either by our actions or those of others—that it comes into sharp focus. This is when stress, discomfort, and cognitive dissonance surge into consciousness.

Imagine always valuing honesty, yet finding yourself in a situation where telling the truth could have significant personal or professional repercussions. Suddenly, you feel a deep and unsettling tension. This discomfort resides in the stark and painful clash between your deeply held value of honesty and the action you are considering.

In these moments—when our values are violated and we feel dissonance—we realize the critical role that values play in our lives. They are not abstract or ornamental; they are visceral and central to our sense of self. The distress we feel at these times is a form of existential alarm, alerting us to the fact that we are on the brink of betraying something fundamental to our identity and maybe even our survival.

This realization can be a profound and transformative experience if we are receptive. It invites us into a space of introspection, where we are compelled to examine the depth of our commitment to our values and the lengths we are willing to go to uphold them. It is an opportunity for realignment and for recommitting to our values, informed by the stark clarity that such moments of tension provide.

In this way, our values are not static; they are dynamic and evolving, shaped and clarified through our lived experiences. They are our silent partners in life's journey, speaking most loudly when we risk losing our way, then guiding us back to our authentic selves and our vision for who we want to be.

THE CORE VALUES OF LIFE AND LIVING THINGS

The story of life's origin teems with theories from various disciplines, including science, religion, and philosophy. The theory of abiogenesis posits that life emerged from simple organic compounds that eventually combined to form complex, self-replicating molecules. In contrast, the panspermia theory suggests that life was seeded from outer space, perhaps through comets or meteorites. Meanwhile, the RNA world hypothesis imagines that the earliest life forms were based on RNA molecules acting as genetic couriers and chemical catalysts.

These theories are contrasted by more spiritual perspectives. Religious doctrines offer divine or supernatural narratives for life's creation, such as the Genesis account in the Christian Bible or the cosmic dance of creation and destruction in Hindu mythology, which is one of my favorites. (If you haven't explored the *Ramayana* or *Mahabharata*, I suggest adding them to your reading list—these sacred texts make *Lord of the Rings* look rather tame in comparison.)

Philosophically, the discourse expands further: vitalism suggests that a life force beyond physical entities exists, and panpsychism considers consciousness, however rudimentary, a universal and primordial feature of all things.

These theories, each with unique perspectives and interpretations, represent humanity's quest to untangle the mystery of life's origin—and meaning.

What we do know is that life, in all its complexity, is guided by a set of core values that enable organisms to survive and thrive. These values, rooted in principles of biology and evolution, are directly responsible for the miracle of our existence.

Let's explore these core values:

Self-Preservation: The innate drive for self-preservation is at the core of every living entity. This value propels an organism's quest for essential resources, such as food and shelter, and its instinct to evade threats. This is the basic tenet for survival—an organism must protect and sustain its own life.

Reproduction: Beyond mere survival, life is about lineage—passing genetic material to successive generations. Reproduction is vital for the continuation of species, and involves elaborate strategies, rituals, and behaviors to secure a mate and produce offspring.

Adaptation: Adaptation is a testament to life's resilience, allowing organisms to modify themselves in response to changing environments. This continual adjustment, honed by natural selection, fuels the spectacular diversity of life on Earth.

Homeostasis: Internal equilibrium, or homeostasis, is paramount. Living organisms perpetually adjust physiological processes to maintain a stable internal environment. This delicate balance supports cellular functions and overall health.

Cooperation: Although competition is prevalent in nature, cooperation is equally important. From symbiotic relationships between species to complex social structures within animal groups, collaborative interactions are abundant and beneficial, enhancing chances of survival and reproduction.

Energy Conservation: Life is a masterful energy economist, and every organism, from single cells to complex creatures, has evolved strategies to optimize energy use. This efficiency is essential for enduring times of scarcity; in humans, it is exemplified by the storage of excess energy in fat. These reserves, housed in adipose tissue, are meticulously managed, ready to be mobilized during times when food intake is low, mirroring adaptive behaviors such as torpor or hibernation seen in other species.

These core values of living organisms are far from mere biological mechanisms; they are the guiding principles that have sculpted the behaviors and adaptations of life forms throughout the eons. By understanding these values, we gain more than knowledge; we foster a profound appreciation for the awe-inspiring diversity and resilience of life on Earth.

A BRIEF HISTORY OF HUMAN VALUES

Imagine a time when our ancestors roamed the earth, when a successful day was measured by the food gathered and the safety of the tribe. Survival wasn't just an individual endeavor; it was a collective one. Our core values were clear: cooperation, sharing, respect for the natural world that sustained us.

Then came the agricultural revolution, and with it, a shift. Our values grew roots, much like the crops we farmed. Stability and resource accumulation became the new measures of wealth. Social structures emerged, with power dynamics that shaped our beliefs and practices. Spirituality was formalized, reinforcing these new values.

Fast-forward to the industrial age, and the landscape of values shifted once more. Efficiency, innovation, individual achievement—these became the currency of progress. Our success was no longer about what we shared, but what we owned, what we knew, and what status we achieved.

In our modern era, the definition of value is as varied as the people who walk this planet. We grapple with a mix of legacy values and contemporary challenges. Yes, we've made incredible strides—longer lifespans, technological marvels, a wealth of knowledge. Yet, we face epidemics of loneliness, mental health crises, and a yearning for purpose that material success alone can't fulfill.

This is our moment of truth. It's time to ask ourselves: What are the values that truly matter to us now? Are they echoes of the past, or are they consciously chosen as guiding stars for our future? That is the purpose of this book.

THE RESEARCH AND STUDY OF VALUES

The study of values spans ages and disciplines, touching every facet of human existence. It is a journey undertaken by prophets, philosophers, scholars, and scientists, each contributing their unique perspective to this ever-evolving narrative. I gratefully acknowledge all who have contributed to humanity's search for meaning and fulfillment. I'm humbled to contribute in my own small way, hopefully shining a light for someone—perhaps you—who is on their own journey of discovery.

Let's now traverse continents and eras, disciplines and cultures, from the earliest inklings of values in ancient wisdom traditions to the methodical inquiries of modern psychology and beyond. In doing so, we will draw a map that connects our past with the present, and the individual with the cosmos.

Ancient Wisdom & Early Texts

The examination of values began not with scientific research but with the narrative wisdom of early human societies. Ancient texts like the Egyptian *Instruction of Amenemope*, the Indian *Vedas*, and the Chinese *Analects of Confucius* are among the first recorded explorations of human values, offering moral guidance based on virtue, justice, and social harmony.

Religious Traditions

The world's major religions, from Christianity and Islam to Buddhism and Hinduism, have been profound shapers of human values. These religious traditions provide moral codes and deeply ingrained systems of values that have shaped societies for millennia, stressing principles like compassion, piety, and justice. They represent some of the earliest systematic attempts to codify what is right and good within a community.

Philosophical Inquiry

Classical Greek philosophers, notably Socrates, Plato, and Aristotle, shifted the exploration of values from the divine to the human domain of reason and debate. Ethics became a central concern for these thinkers, who sought to understand virtue and the good life through reason and dialogue. This tradition of ethical philosophy continued through the Enlightenment with philosophers such as Kant and Mill, who offered diverging views on moral duty and the greatest good.

Modern Psychology

The 20th century saw values enter the realm of science with the advent of psychology. Psychologists like Abraham Maslow, who proposed the hierarchy of human needs, and Milton Rokeach, who developed a values survey to systematically study the guiding principles in people's lives, brought the study of values into the empirical framework of modern science. Their contributions laid the groundwork for understanding how values shape human behavior and mental health.

Cultural Anthropology and Sociology

These disciplines have expanded our understanding of values as culturally and socially constructed entities. Anthropologists like Clifford Geertz and sociologists such as Emile Durkheim have studied values as integral to the social fabric of different communities, revealing the wide variety of forms that human values can take depending on cultural context.

Contemporary Interdisciplinary Approaches

Today, the study of values is a vibrant interdisciplinary field. Behavioral economists, combining insights from psychology and economics, examine how values influence decision-making. Environmental ethicists consider the values that underlie our treatment of the natural world. Bioethicists grapple with the values involved in emerging biotechnologies, particularly in healthcare. AI ethicists study how to optimize AI's beneficial impact while reducing the risk of adverse outcomes. Space ethicists, a relatively new addition, evaluate the moral aspects of space exploration and colonization, questioning our responsibilities not just on Earth but also as we extend our reach into the cosmos. They challenge us to consider the impact of our extraterrestrial endeavors on other worlds and the universe at large, ensuring that the expansion of human activity beyond Earth is conducted with foresight and respect for cosmic environments and potential life.

As we consider this rich history of values research, what stands out is the enduring human quest for understanding the values that guide our lives. From ancient sages to modern scientists, this journey reflects our deep need to understand not just how we act but how we should act.

WHERE DO INDIVIDUAL VALUES COME FROM?

It's clear that culture shapes values and beliefs, but what makes our personal core values so unique? Are they the result of our genetic makeup, upbringing, life stage, or individual experiences? Let's explore how core values emerge and crystallize in individuals.

The Genetic Influence

Behavioral genetics suggests that our temperament and personality traits are influenced by our genetic makeup. Through twin studies, researchers like Thomas Bouchard have shown that identical twins raised apart still share remarkable similarities in their attitudes and values, suggesting a genetic component.

The Neurobiological Aspect

The interplay between our prefrontal cortex, the brain's command center for decision-making and complex thought, and our limbic system, home to the amygdala and hippocampus, shapes values-based behavior. The prefrontal cortex not only governs our choices but also moderates our social behaviors and ethical reasoning, contributing to value formation. Meanwhile, the amygdala's processing of emotional responses, in concert with the hippocampus's role in forming and retrieving memories, determines the significance we place on these values. Together, they form a neurobiological network that assigns weight to our values based on past experiences and emotional learning, contextualizing our individual value systems within a broader social and environmental framework.

The Role of Early Life and Parents

Social learning theory, developed by Albert Bandura, suggests that individuals learn by observing important figures, usually parents, in their lives. The values instilled during early childhood often persist into adulthood.

Cultural Impact

Different cultures prioritize different values. Geert Hofstede's cultural dimensions theory offers insight into how culture shapes our values. For example, individualism is more valued in Western societies, whereas Eastern cultures lean toward collectivism.

Experiential Learning

Personal experiences shape our understanding of what is important. For example, Viktor Frankl's logotherapy is based on his concentration camp experiences, which led him to value meaning and purpose above all else.

Social and Peer Influence

The need for social acceptance and belongingness, as proposed in Maslow's Hierarchy of Needs, can cause people to adopt the values of their peer group, even if these differ from earlier influences.

Cognitive Development

According to Jean Piaget's theory of cognitive development, our moral understanding evolves over time as we mature, which can lead to shifts in our values.

The Evolutionary Angle

From an evolutionary perspective, some values, like cooperation, could have conferred survival benefits, as proposed by theories like kin selection and reciprocal altruism.

The Rational Choice

Some people choose their values based on philosophical, ethical, or religious frameworks, actively and intentionally evaluating belief systems before adopting them.

The Integrated Hypothesis

Most likely, our values result from an intricate web of these influences. This integrated hypothesis allows for a more nuanced understanding of value formation, embracing the complexity of human psychology and behavior.

2

WHY DO VALUES MATTER?

CONSIDER THE STORY of your life. Your story reflects the chain of daily decisions you have made and the resulting actions you have taken. Values are central to your decisions. They serve as an internal compass guiding you through a world that is perpetually changing, often overwhelming, and certainly uncertain.

Your values are like an algorithm in a GPS that continually evaluates which roads will provide an optimal route to your destination. However, they don't just scan for speed; they consider what is most important. Your destination might be parenthood, career progression, or philanthropy; whatever the case may be, it is your values that help you navigate towards this destination, avoiding paths that may lead to distress and nudging you toward what matters.

For example, you might realize that you have not been living in alignment with your value of physical fitness. You resolve to get fit, but there are many potential routes:

- Join a CrossFit club and participate in three half-hour sessions per week
- Sign up with a yoga studio and practice for three hours per week
- Take up long-distance running

You might think that your final decision is based purely on preference. But if you enjoy all three activities, how will you decide? If you value time with *family*, you might forgo long-distance running and choose the convenience of CrossFit. If you value *peace*, you will likely choose a yoga studio over a high-intensity workout or hitting the road. If you value *freedom*, then marathons might be your thing. It is your underlying values that ultimately offer the route to your destination.

Especially in times of hardship, when life's pressures and expectations weigh heavily upon us, our values can serve as torches in the darkness. They clarify what is truly important, inspiring us to act accordingly. When we follow a route charted by our values, we are not merely enduring life's trials; we are actively engaging with them. This is called *values alignment*, or *integrity*.

Values-aligned action leads to fulfillment, which is essential for personal resilience and well-being. In a society where external achievements are often hailed as the ultimate success, living in harmony with our values offers a more reflective, internal form of accomplishment. It is the satisfaction that stems from knowing we are being authentic and respecting our true selves, both in tranquil and turbulent times.

In this sense, our values are the architects of our fulfillment, and the silent co-authors of a life that is not just "good," but also profoundly, resonantly *meaningful*.

VALUES MAKE US HAPPY

My favorite definition of happiness was given to me by Dr. Sven Hansen, founder of the Resilience Institute. He said, "Happiness is a temporary relief from suffering." For most people plugged into our modern world, suffering—most often in the form of stress—is a common adversary, and the pursuit of happiness can feel like an endless maze. However, the solution to both might be simpler than we think—it could be closely tied to understanding and aligning with our core values.

Psychology researchers have discovered the profound effect our values can have on our well-being. For instance, a study conducted by

Edward Deci and Richard Ryan, pioneers of the self-determination theory, found that, when people live in alignment with their values, they are more likely to experience a higher quality of life, with less stress and greater happiness. This is because living according to our values acts as a psychological stabilizer.

Consider stress, which is a physiological response evolved to protect us from immediate danger. Today's stressors are more likely to be psychological—work pressures, family conflicts, or societal expectations—than physical threats like lions, wolves, or marauding enemy tribes. A risk we often don't recognize is how, when our actions are at odds with our values, the discord generates constant, low-level stress, like a computer program running in the background, consuming mental energy. This is called chronic—rather than acute—stress, and it is strongly linked to inflammation, weakened immunity, and mental health disorders. Living in line with our values eases this internal conflict. We make decisions with more clarity and conviction, freeing ourselves from the exhausting pull of indecision and second-guessing.

Research by psychologist Steven Hayes, founder of Acceptance and Commitment Therapy (ACT), emphasizes that engaging in values-driven activities—such as practicing gratitude, kindness, and mindfulness—significantly supports fulfillment. When our actions resonate with our values, each decision we make and each action we take feels meaningful and satisfying, thus contributing to a more enduring form of happiness.

It is clear that values can guide us through life's complexities, reducing the friction that generates stress and pointing us toward actions that fulfill us, making happiness more accessible. In this light, our values are not words or concepts; they are practical tools for a more focused, less stressful, and happier life. They are not luxuries but necessities for our modern minds and spirits—the keys to a life of less stress and greater fulfillment.

VALUES GIVE CLARITY

We have more options available to us than ever before. Research shows that having too many choices leads to decisions made out of convenience, peer pressure, or fleeting desires rather than what is important—a phenomenon known as the "paradox of choice." As a result, the modern abundance meant to empower us can inadvertently distance us from our authentic selves, compromising the integrity of our decisions and actions. On the flip side, we sometimes get lost on the back streets of life without realizing that alternative routes are available.

Having a clear set of values is like carrying a high-powered LED headtorch while on a night expedition. Without the headtorch, we're stumbling in the dark, often selecting the path of least resistance. Switch the torch on, and suddenly, we can delineate shapes, identify pathways, and avoid obstacles. Turned on—or brought to the forefront of decision-making—our values cut through the fog of uncertainty and illuminate paths that, while they may still be challenging, are clearly defined and aligned with what is most important. As my mentor, Ian Hutchinson, frequently says, "Clarity creates control."

Properly engaged, our core values act as powerful lenses through which we perceive and interact with the world. When faced with choices, large or small, it is our values that help us to quickly and confidently discern which options are in alignment with our authentic selves. Instead of becoming paralyzed by the many possible directions one could take, our values simplify these decisions by eliminating options that don't resonate. It's a clarifying process, removing the extraneous noise and leaving behind only those choices that are congruent with who we are and who we strive to be.

For example, if honesty is a core value, then the decision to speak the truth—even when uncomfortable—is natural. If compassion guides our lives, then our actions towards others, particularly in tense situations, will be infused with understanding and empathy rather than hostility. When we establish what matters most to us, the ambiguous becomes clear, and what was once a branching path of endless options becomes a focused route that feels right and resonates with our inner self.

In this way, our values are not just abstract ideals; they are practical tools for living a more purposeful and less chaotic life. They are both an internal compass and a headtorch, pointing us in the direction that aligns with our deepest convictions and helping us map a path.

In the quest for a clear and meaningful life, our values are our most trusted guides. They clarify our path, simplify our choices, and instill in us the confidence to navigate the complex and often uncertain journey of life with purpose and without regret.

Steve Jobs famously said, "You can't connect the dots looking forward; you can only connect them looking backwards. So, you have to trust that the dots will somehow connect in your future. You have to trust in something—your gut, destiny, life, karma, whatever. This approach has never let me down, and it has made all the difference in my life."

Here's what I would add: Don't trust destiny or karma. Trust your values. Steve valued innovation, focus and excellence—and look at the impact he made.

VALUES HELP YOU SAY NO

Now, let's talk about the power of saying "no." When your values are clear, this two-letter word becomes an essential tool for shaping your life according to your own terms. It's not just a rejection or a denial; it's a valiant act.

As established in *The Power of Saying No* by Vanessa Patrick, PhD, this vital skill conserves personal energy and time, ensures alignment with core values, prevents burnout from overcommitment, enhances self-worth, sharpens decision-making, fortifies relationships, and paves the way for meaningful opportunities and growth. This academic perspective echoes a sentiment often attributed to successful individuals like Warren Buffett, who once remarked, "The difference between successful people and really successful people is that really successful people say no to almost everything."

Think about it this way: if work-life balance is one of your values, declining an invitation to a work-related event on your day off is not just about saying no to your employer—it's about saying *yes* to your well-being and personal life.

Your values empower you to create boundaries that respect your time, energy, and emotional space. By understanding and applying your values, you're not just navigating life's challenges; you're consciously shaping your life's direction, saying no to pathways that ultimately will lead you to suffering, regret, or boredom, and yes to those that will lead to fulfillment.

In the next section, we will identify your core values. They're your guides, pointing the way to improved relationships and a life that resonates with who you truly are.

3

DISCOVER YOUR VALUES

IN ANY ACADEMIC or philosophical endeavor, the crafting of
models and frameworks is an exercise in simplification. The aim
is to distill abstract or complex concepts into accessible forms,
making them easier to understand. Even well-regarded models like
Maslow's Hierarchy of Needs have faced their fair share of critique
and challenges over the years. Remember, models aren't crafted for
nuance; they're designed to provide a framework through which we
can view and interpret the world. As fewer people rely on traditional
values frameworks, such as those prescribed by religious doctrines,
we can benefit greatly from having reference guides for increasing
self-awareness and supporting decisive action.

The Values Pyramid offers a perspective on how values can shift
based on context and how consistently applying these values may
lead to fulfillment. It's essential, however, to emphasize that such
frameworks don't claim universality. An individual could very well
be operating from a survival standpoint, as situated at the base of the
pyramid, yet be making impactful and fulfilling contributions. Think
of a doctor working in a conflict zone or a firefighter saving lives as a
building collapses.

So, fully acknowledging the messy nature of life, I present the
Values Pyramid, a model developed with input from academics, data-
driven insights, and analysis.

THE VALUES PYRAMID

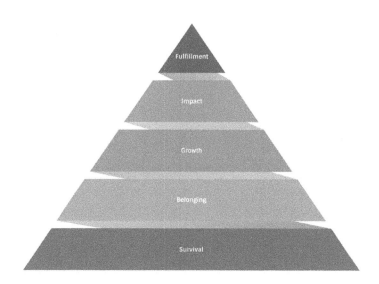

At the base of the pyramid lie our Survival values. Here, we find the fundamental necessities for human existence: security, food, water, and shelter. Financial security is included in here because, without it, most of us quickly descend toward hardship or poverty. This financial security may come from work, family, a spouse, government support, or other means.

As we ascend, we reach the layer of Belonging. This refers primarily to love, defined broadly enough to encompass our family bonds, friendships, and intimate relationships. It is the warmth of being part of a community and a society where people are treated with respect and fairness. A sense of belonging to planet Earth is the reason that sustainability is included here.

Climbing further, we encounter Growth values. This is where we find the passion for learning and growth in education and knowledge. It is here that we also experience the pursuit of physical and mental well-being. Achievement and competence are important aspects of growth, marking our striving for mastery and success in our personal and professional lives.

As we near the pyramid's peak, we enter the realm of Impact. In this stratum, the primary values are status and influence. High levels of competence often result in increased autonomy and a shift towards a focus on work-life balance. Alongside this, we grapple with wealth and material success, the tangible markers of our journey.

At the top of the pyramid, we arrive at Fulfillment. This is where we discover meaning and practice gratitude. Many seek a connection to something greater than themselves, whether spiritual, community, or a sense of unity with the universe. Becoming a steward for our planet and supporting others are common paths to the experience of fulfillment.

In this hierarchical construct, the most foundational values act as the bedrock upon which we build our lives. When these foundational values are threatened, they naturally demand our attention. As we secure each layer, we become free to explore and prioritize higher, possibly more fulfilling and enriching values.

When I think back to my journey, survival values were often lurking close to the surface of my reality and influencing my behavior accordingly. As a child, there were times when there wasn't much food in the fridge or kitchen cupboards. My sister and I once resorted to selling clothing on the beachfront to buy groceries. The scarcity mindset is challenging to unravel, and for many people who are born into difficult economic circumstances, abundance—or even stability—is an alien concept. Within this mindset, our view of the world is necessarily limited to the next meal or paycheck. When I arrived in London, I had nothing. My small suitcase, packed by my beloved grandmother, was full of the warmest clothing she could find. I arrived during a heatwave. But I quickly found a job and room, scraped by for those first weeks, gradually made friends, and met someone who eventually became a wonderful girlfriend.

My motivation increased when I saw how others achieved success, and so I started buying books, learning, and improving myself at work and through physical fitness. I received promotions for my dedication, then saved up enough to go backpacking for two whole months, spending a summer meandering through Turkey, Greece, Italy, and Spain. I soaked up history and sunshine and found immense fulfillment in the adventure.

You can see how this phase of my journey ascended the pyramid, from survival all the way to fulfillment. But the Values Pyramid is not a rigid structure. It is a fluid, living framework that attempts to mirror the journeys of human life. Our values are deeply personal, and this pyramid is a way to introspect about what we hold dear, what we prioritize, and how we might strive for a deeper, more harmonious alignment with what matters. Remember, we have values across the pyramid at all times, but are we always conscious of them? Are they guiding our behavior, leading to fulfillment?

Here is another way to look at the Values Pyramid, featuring the meta-categories—or states of being—survive, engage, and thrive.

Let's explore each of these meta-categories in more detail.

1. **Survive:** This foundational state focuses on meeting our essential needs for security, health, and resources—everything that's necessary to maintain life and personal safety.

2. **Engage:** This stage represents the awakening and energizing of one's potential, encompassing learning, curiosity, and the development of physical, emotional, and mental capacities. It's also where individuals begin to actively pursue their interests, experiencing the joys of personal achievements and relationships.

3. **Thrive:** In the "Thrive" stage, individuals reach a level of flourishing that extends beyond the self. This stage is about making a meaningful impact, achieving a sense of fulfillment, and contributing to the well-being of others. It's the stage where one's growth and engagement translate into lasting influence and legacy.

Now it is time to discover what is most important to you. Maybe you already have an inkling, or perhaps you have your values printed on a poster beside your desk; maybe you have no idea whatsoever.

I'm here to help, and I have created several ways for you to get started with the discovery process.

In this section we'll explore:

- Using fulfillment as your guide
- Exploring the values of people that you admire
- The Values App
- The Values List (for those who don't want to use an app)
- Making values actionable
- The optimal number of values and how to rank them

We'll also look at intrinsic versus extrinsic values, means versus end values, and lots more. I have included a diverse range of tools and methodologies for you to try out. Some are more cognitive and some more intuitive. Please treat this section as a workbook; feel free to skip over tools that don't resonate and use those that do. This is your discovery process. Have fun!

USING FULFILLMENT AS YOUR GUIDE

Fulfillment is derived from meaningful action, which, in turn, is directed by values-based decision-making. So, let's start at the top of the Values Pyramid and reflect on what has brought you the most fulfillment on your journey so far.

I'll share mine as an example. My fulfillment has come from:

- **Adventure:** Times when I set off into the unknown with no map or plan.
- **Creativity:** Giving a creative gift to the world, be it a book, blog post, movie, digital platform, or photograph.
- **Fitness:** Feeling physically strong, flexible, and ready to push my limits. Also, experiencing the high of intense exertion.
- **Love:** Experiencing love for family, friends, colleagues, and, sometimes, all living beings and the world.
- **Peace:** Achieving moments of deep rest without guilt. Allocating time and space for introspection and reflection.

Remember that you can discover your values through meaningful activities, like socializing (friendship), mastering a new skill (learning) or doing something grand like volunteering at an orphanage (altruism).

Here are some examples:

Successfully completing a major project at work

Core Value: Achievement
The successful completion of a significant work project fulfills the core value of achievement, reflecting a dedication to goals and the

satisfaction derived from overcoming challenges and contributing value to one's organization.

Conquering a fear of heights

Core Value: Courage
Overcoming a fear of heights epitomizes the core value of courage, providing fulfillment through personal growth, the overcoming of limitations, and the expansion of one's comfort zone, enabling new experiences and opportunities.

Learning computer programming

Core Value: Learning
The process of learning computer programming signifies a commitment to self-improvement, mastery, and the ongoing pursuit of skill development in an ever-evolving field.

Starting a side hustle

Core Value: Autonomy
Launching a side hustle—or founding a startup—represents the core value of autonomy, offering fulfillment through the pursuit of personal passions, the creation of value, and the empowerment that comes from building something of one's own.

Saving up a deposit for your first home

Core Value: Responsibility
Saving for a deposit on a first home embodies the core value of responsibility, demonstrating a commitment to financial planning, foresight, and the fulfillment derived from achieving a major life milestone through discipline and perseverance.

> **Action:** Spend 10 minutes writing down the events, achievements, habits, or behaviors you are most proud of or grateful for, then identify the values underpinning each item. For example, if you wrote down "seeing my child grow up," that reflects the values of family and care. If you need help connecting what fulfills you with your deeper values, use the Values List on page 28.

VALUES OF PEOPLE YOU ADMIRE

Take a moment to consider the heroes, mentors, and inspirational figures who have shaped your worldview. What are the qualities in them that you respect and admire? More often than not, the values of those we look up to are a mirror reflecting our own values. Here's an exercise to guide you:

- Reflect on the people you admire.
- Identify the qualities that draw you to them.
- Write down the specific values they embody that resonate with you.

To spark your reflection, here's a list of ten notable people from diverse backgrounds, along with three values they are widely recognized for:

1. **Nelson Mandela:** Resilience, Leadership, Equality

2. **Malala Yousafzai:** Courage, Education, Women's Rights

3. **Mahatma Gandhi:** Non-violence, Truth, Self-discipline

4. **Marie Curie:** Perseverance, Intellectual Curiosity, Scientific Integrity

5. **Martin Luther King Jr.:** Justice, Compassion, Community

6. **Simone Biles:** Determination, Excellence, Mental Health Advocacy

7. **Elon Musk:** Innovation, Ambition, Sustainability

8. **Ruth Bader Ginsburg:** Justice, Equality, Legal Acumen

9. **Dalai Lama:** Compassion, Spirituality, Peace

10. **Serena Williams:** Competitiveness, Resilience, Excellence

The values you admire in others are both a mirror and a compass pointing you toward your own North Star.

> **Action:** Jot down the names of three people you admire and the values you think they embody. If any of the values resonate strongly with you, write them on your list.

USE THE VALUES APP

Now, it's time to put down this book and pick up your phone or flip open your laptop. I have created an app that is designed to help you discover your core values. It's simple and easy. Simply scan this QR code or visit: startwithvalues.com/app.

Once you're done, you can skip the following section and move directly to Extrinsic versus Intrinsic Values on page 31. If you don't want to use a digital app, read on.

THE VALUES LIST

While you may have already discovered some core values by considering what has brought you fulfillment or via the people you admire, it's time to dive deeper.

Please review the following categories and select the values that resonate. Think about how you are rather than how you would like to be. Note that I don't include survival values in this discovery process, as I want you to focus on values that will help you feel engaged, and to thrive. However, I do explore the survival layer of values on page 48.

Please select a maximum of three values from each category. Remember, the point is to uncover the essence of what matters most to you rather than selecting everything you desire.

Belonging

- Love
- Friendship
- Respect
- Fairness
- Community
- Empathy
- Kindness
- Intimacy
- Family
- Teamwork
- Collaboration
- Inclusion

Growth

- Learning
- Achievement
- Curiosity
- Balance
- Physical Fitness
- Mental Fitness
- Skill Mastery
- Resilience
- Adaptability
- Creativity
- Courage
- Honesty

Impact

- Influence
- Status
- Wealth
- Credibility
- Risk-Taking
- Autonomy
- Leadership
- Advocacy
- Visibility
- Authority
- Accomplishment
- Reputation

Fulfillment

- Peace
- Gratitude
- Wisdom
- Spirituality
- Social Contribution
- Nature Stewardship
- Vocation
- Philanthropy
- Transcendence
- Legacy
- Altruism
- Awe

Action: Transfer your selected values, along with any others you identified earlier, onto a fresh list.

YOUR TOP FIVE VALUES

Now that you've compiled a list of values, let's prune them down to your core five. You must be willing to valiantly defend each value and allow it to serve as a guiding light in decision-making.

Refine your list by subjecting each value to the following tests:

1. **Essential to Your Identity:** These are values that, if removed from your life, would change the essence of who you are. They're non-negotiable and deeply intertwined with your sense of self. Test each of the values by asking, "Could I live without {value} in my life?" If the answer is yes, then cross it off the list.

2. **Gut Check:** Intuition or gut feeling is a powerful indicator. As you review your selected values, which ones evoke a strong emotional response? Which ones feel like they "fit?" Trust your instincts.

3. **Day-to-Day Alignment:** Reflect on your daily actions and decisions. Which values are consistently present? Sometimes, the values we live by daily are so ingrained that we overlook them. But their consistency is a testament to their importance in our lives. Ask yourself, "Do I practice {value} every day?"

4. **Future Projection:** Consider your goals, aspirations, and the life you want to lead. Which values align with that vision? Ask yourself, "Does the future version of me prioritize {value}?" This is especially important if you have been living in survival mode.

5. **The Elimination Test:** If you struggle to decide between a few values, consider doing an elimination test. Imagine having to give up one value at a time. Which one would you be more willing to part with, even if just slightly? This process can help you discern the relative importance of each value.

6. **Seek External Insight:** Sometimes, discussing your values with a trusted friend or mentor can provide clarity. They might offer insights into how they perceive your values or ask probing questions that help you reflect deeper.

Remember, identifying core values isn't about choosing what's most aspirational but about recognizing what's authentically you.

It's a mix of introspection, reflection, and a bit of soul-searching. And as you evolve, it's entirely natural for your values to shift or change.

> **Action:** What are your top five values? Identify and write them down on a blank piece of paper before we continue the journey.

EXTRINSIC VERSUS INTRINSIC VALUES

The next step is to understand the difference between intrinsic and extrinsic values. Both have their place, but they serve different roles and are influenced by a range of factors, some of which are within our control and others which aren't.

While extrinsic values are shaped by the external world—think societal norms, peer pressure, or cultural expectations—intrinsic values are pillars supporting our sense of self.

I hold two intrinsic values close to my heart: creativity and kindness. Living these values makes me feel authentic and true to myself. It's worth noting that these intrinsic values could be viewed as adaptive strategies, honed over countless human interactions since my early years. The more I exhibit creativity and kindness, the richer my interactions become, leading to positive outcomes. This creates a reinforcing cycle where favorable responses from others further cement these values in my behavior.

The satisfaction you get from acting based on intrinsic values comes from the act itself, not from what it will earn you in external rewards or recognition. Researchers like Edward Deci and Richard Ryan, architects of the previously mentioned self-determination theory, discovered a fascinating blueprint: aligning with intrinsic values doesn't just resonate internally; it also echoes outwards, boosting well-being, resilience, and performance. Extrinsic values, on the other hand, are oriented towards external rewards or recognition. Think about values like wealth, social status, or physical attractiveness. While there's nothing inherently wrong with these values, they often depend on external circumstances or other people's judgments, making them somewhat precarious. If your well-being or self-esteem relies heavily on these, you will struggle in the face of rejection or failure.

The interesting thing to note is that, while both types of values can contribute to a fulfilling life, we generally have more control over our intrinsic values. You can always develop your capacity for patience, kindness, or creativity, regardless of your external circumstances. Extrinsic values often depend on factors outside your control, like economic conditions or approval by a gatekeeper figure.

So, as you prioritize your core values, consider leaning more towards intrinsic values. These are the values that you can act on every day, no matter what life throws at you. They empower you to focus on what you can control, providing a more stable foundation for well-being, and making your journey more fulfilling.

INTRINSIC VERSUS EXTRINSIC VALUE TEST

To help you clarify the nature of your core values, we've developed a formula that assesses motivation origin, fulfillment source, consistency across contexts, and independence from external validation. By answering targeted questions, you can determine whether a value is primarily intrinsic, extrinsic, or a blend of both. (Feel free to skip to the next section if formulas are not your thing.)

For each value on your list, ask the following four questions and write down the letter I or E beside it.

Motivation Origin: Does the motivation come from within (personal satisfaction, joy, inner peace) or from outside (recognition, rewards, external approval)?

- Intrinsic Indicator (I): Motivation comes from within.
- Extrinsic Indicator (E): Motivation comes from external factors.

Fulfillment Source: Is fulfillment derived from the act itself or from the outcome and external recognition it brings?

- Intrinsic (I): Fulfillment from the act itself.
- Extrinsic (E): Fulfillment from outcomes or recognition.

Consistency Across Contexts: Would you prioritize this value even if external circumstances change dramatically?

- Intrinsic (I): Yes, it's consistent.
- Extrinsic (E): No, it's dependent on circumstances.

Independence from External Validation: Do you need external validation to find this value meaningful?

- Intrinsic (I): No need for external validation.
- Extrinsic (E): Requires external validation.

Scoring: For each value, tally your responses by counting the number of I's and E's.

Outcome:

- Mostly I's: The value is primarily Intrinsic.
- Mostly E's: The value is primarily Extrinsic.

Let's test the formula on some typical values.

Example 1: I am passionate about learning.

Value: Learning

- **Motivation Origin:** I—Intrinsic—motivation comes from the joy of discovery and understanding new things.

- **Fulfillment Source:** I—Intrinsic—fulfillment is derived from the process of learning itself.
- **Consistency Across Contexts:** I—Intrinsic—I would pursue learning regardless of changes in external circumstances.
- **Independence from External Validation:** I—Intrinsic—I do not need external validation to find learning meaningful.

Scoring:

- Intrinsic: 4
- Extrinsic: 0

Outcome: The value of learning in this example is definitively Intrinsic.

Example 2: I'm pursuing promotions to elevate my status.

Value: Status

- **Motivation Origin:** E—Extrinsic—motivation comes from the desire for higher status and salary.
- **Fulfillment Source:** E—Extrinsic—fulfillment is derived from receiving the promotion and recognition by peers and superiors.
- **Consistency Across Contexts:** E—Extrinsic—the importance of pursuing promotions may vary with changes in the workplace or career aspirations.
- **Independence from External Validation:** E—Extrinsic—requires recognition and validation from others to find the pursuit meaningful.

Scoring:

- Intrinsic: 0
- Extrinsic: 4

Outcome: The value of status in this example is definitively Extrinsic.

Example 3: I want to look and feel good.

Value: Physical Fitness

- Motivation Origin: E—Extrinsic—motivation comes from wanting to look good and receive compliments.
- Fulfillment Source: I—Intrinsic—fulfillment is derived from the feeling of health, vitality, and personal well-being.
- Consistency Across Contexts: I—Intrinsic—I would stay fit even if no one noticed because of the personal health benefits.
- Independence from External Validation: E—Extrinsic—my current exercise routine is shaped by my desire to meet societal standards and external perceptions of beauty.

Scoring:

- Intrinsic: 2
- Extrinsic: 2

Outcome: The value of physical fitness in this example has an even split, indicating it holds both Intrinsic and Extrinsic elements for the individual. This balance suggests that, while part of the commitment to fitness is driven by personal health and satisfaction, there's also a significant influence from external validation.

> **Action:** Revisit your list of values. How many intrinsic and extrinsic values have you written down? I recommend leaning toward intrinsic values. Now is a good time to reflect on what will ultimately drive greatest fulfillment over the course of your life. Adjust your list based on this exercise. You may reintroduce a value (or two) that you removed earlier to replace a primarily extrinsic value.

MEANS VERSUS END VALUES

Some values are steppingstones—we call these "means values." They are like the rungs on a ladder, necessary for climbing towards our goals. Means values are about the 'how'—e.g. learning, resilience, and collaboration—the behaviors and practices through which we navigate our journey.

Then there are "end values," which are the reasons we climb the ladder in the first place. They represent our ultimate destinations—e.g. legacy, peace, social contribution. End values define the 'why'—the core motivations that give our lives meaning and direction.

How do these concepts fit within the structure of our values pyramid? The Survival layer is where we clearly see means values at play. Here, the focus is on securing the necessities of life through actions and behaviors that ensure our basic needs are met. It's where practicality often overshadows aspiration, and our values are focused on maintaining stability, security, and health.

As we ascend to the Belonging and Growth layers, we begin to blend means with end values. The values here serve dual purposes— they are part of both the journey and the destination.

Reaching the Impact and Fulfillment layers is where our end values genuinely shine. At this point, our focus is on status, altruism, peace, and wisdom. Our means values serve our end values, as the habits we've formed and the actions we've taken culminate in achieving our full potential.

Understanding the interplay between means and end values helps us navigate life with intention. Most of us will have a scattering of values across the Values Pyramid. If you are too biased towards one or two of the layers, take a wide-angle perspective and see if you can find a way to balance the how—means values—with your why—end values.

Action: Reviewing your list, can you determine how many are means and how many are end values? If you are too biased toward means values—just like extrinsic values—it might be worth a deeper look. Check to see whether you're really clear on those deeper, lifelong values that will contribute to a lasting sense of fulfillment. If necessary, recalibrate your list to include a few more end values. You will be using your values to guide important decisions, so ensure they are profoundly resonant.

VALUES MUST ENABLE ACTION

Now, it's time to test your selected values by turning the words into practical behaviors. Take the value of love, for instance. Love is a wonderful value to have, but it's also a bit abstract. You might say you value love, but what does that mean in the context of your day-to-day life? I interviewed a world-leading anthropologist and relationship expert, Dr. Anna Machin, on my podcast, and even she said that there is no clear definition of love. So how can you live in alignment with such an ambiguous—yet undoubtedly powerful—value?

Entertain a bit of neuro-linguistic programming. The concept of "love" can be transformed from a static noun into a kinetic verb, "loving," to emphasize action and ongoing engagement. This simple linguistic shift changes the value from a static concept into a dynamic action. Instead of simply valuing "love," you aim to be "loving." Then, you can set an intention like, "Tonight, I will be a loving father," transforming your value into a concrete, actionable behavior.

Why does this matter? Actionable values can be incorporated into your daily routine, and research rooted in behavioral psychology supports the effectiveness of taking deliberate, actionable steps. The concept of "behavioral activation" emphasizes that small specific actions often create a snowball effect, leading to broader emotional and psychological improvements. It's a bit like the SMART goals framework, which advises that objectives be Specific, Measurable, Achievable, Relevant, and Time-bound. In fact, by making values actionable in the SMART way, you're not just setting intentions; you're cementing the belief that these values can be lived and experienced. It's about operationalizing values into your routine, which in turn, reinforces your belief in their feasibility and your commitment to them.

Let's explore some examples of SMART Values:

Example 1: Health

Specific: Instead of vaguely aiming to be "healthy," specify what aspect of health you are focusing on. For example, "I will focus on cardiovascular health."

Measurable: How will you measure improvement? "I will run for at least 30 minutes, three times a week."

Achievable: Is this feasible given your current health status and schedule? "Yes, I can fit in 30-minute running sessions three times a week."

Relevant: Does this goal align with your broader life values and objectives? "Yes, maintaining good cardiovascular health is critical for my overall well-being and longevity."

Time-bound: When will you evaluate your progress? "I will track my running sessions for the next two months."

Example 2: Learning

Specific: What type of learning are you focusing on? "I will focus on learning Python programming."

Measurable: How will you measure your progress? "I will complete one Python project every two weeks."

Achievable: Can you realistically achieve this? "Yes, I have basic programming knowledge and can spend 5 hours a week on this."

Relevant: Does this align with your broader life goals? "Yes, learning Python will add to my skill set and improve my job prospects."

Time-bound: By when do you want to achieve this? "I aim to have completed six Python projects in the next three months."

Test each of your values as a verb. Can you actively practice each one every day? This approach will not only make your values resonate more deeply with you but also empower you to live them out in meaningful ways. Later in this book, I will dive deeper into other tools for living in alignment with your values, including the power of micro-habits.

> **Action:** Can you turn each of your values into a verb? Can you apply the SMART framework to attach a specific and time-bound action to each of your values?

THE RULE OF THREE

Leonardo da Vinci said, "Simplicity is the ultimate sophistication."

Antoine de Saint-Exupéry, the author of *The Little Prince*, said, "Perfection is achieved, not when there is nothing more to add, but when there is nothing left to take away."

I think you know where I'm going with this. How many values are on your list right now? You might have selected five or even ten values. That's too many!

It's time to sharpen the sword, prune the tree, or polish the diamond (pick whichever metaphor works for you). This process can be uncomfortable, but it will give you clarity. Remember the three C's: "Clarity creates control."

How many values are optimal? Researchers, corporate consultants, authors, and philosophers have different ideas when it comes to the number of values we should select. Note that I say "select" as if you can shop for values as you might shop for shoes. In actuality, we're not selecting values; we're unearthing them. They're like diamonds in a rocky substrate, and our job is to carefully extract, shape, polish, and wear them.

As with jewelry, when it comes to core values, less is more (unless you value *bling*). You might be tempted to have lots of values—integrity, love, freedom, health, success, sustainability, family—it could go on. These are likely to be ideals. Honing in on three—or even two—core values is more effective for a focused, meaningful life. You might wonder why. After all, shouldn't we exemplify a broad spectrum of values? While nice in theory, the reality is that spreading yourself too thin will dilute your efforts and lead to choice overload. If you're juggling a dozen core values, chances are you'll find it hard to make consistently aligned decisions. This doesn't mean that other values are unimportant; rather, leveraging a few enables you to act with speed, clarity, and conviction.

Think about it this way: When everything is a priority, nothing is a priority. The Pareto principle, often known as the 80/20 rule, suggests that 80% of your outcomes come from 20% of your efforts. For our purposes, this means that a few core values should guide the majority of your actions and decisions. They should become pillars that support the architecture of your life, making it easier to prioritize, decide, and understand the trade-offs you're willing to make.

Let's explore the "Rule of Three," which is a testament to the universal appeal of patterns and rhythm in human cognition. Whether in politics, literature, or design, this rule suggests that triads—whether they be concepts, words, or visuals—are inherently engaging, satisfying, and memorable. In the realm of communication, the trifecta strategy serves to emphasize points, craft cadence, and enhance retention. Consider Julius Caesar's "Veni, vidi, vici" (I came, I saw, I conquered) or Abraham Lincoln's "government of the people, by the people, for the people."

Comedians also often rely on the rule of three, using two similar items to set up a pattern, then humorously breaking that pattern with the third item. One common comedic technique is Expectation, Reinforcement, and Surprise. Here's an example:

1. "I bought a new jacket."

2. "It's stylish and comfortable."

3. "And it comes with a free midlife crisis."

As kids, we learn our ABCs, and most stories—including those about three little pigs, bears, sisters, witches, or wishes—have a three-part sequence: beginning, middle, and end.

It is much easier to remember three core values than a laundry list of words that is likely to cause analysis paralysis, if not ultimately forgotten.

Now it's your turn. We're going to trim your list of values to three. Here's how.

1. **Intuitive First Pass:** Quickly skim through your list and highlight or circle the values that immediately jump out to you. Trust your gut feeling.

2. **Visualization Exercise:** Close your eyes and imagine your ideal self in five years. Which values are guiding this future version of you?

3. **The Five Whys:** For each value that stands out to you, ask yourself, "Why is this important to me?" five times in succession. This technique deeply probes your underlying reasons and helps build awareness of what motivates you.

4. **Value Pairing:** Compare two values and ask yourself, "If I could only live by one of these values for the rest of my life, which would it be?" This will help you prioritize.

5. **Daily Reflection:** Over a week, reflect each day on which values were most present or lacking in your actions and decisions. This can shed light on what's important to you.

6. **Consult Trusted Individuals:** Sometimes an outside perspective can provide clarity. Discuss your values list with friends, family, or mentors. They might be able to offer insights on what values they see you embodying most.

7. **Crisis Scenario:** Imagine you're in a challenging situation. Which values would guide your actions? The ones that instinctively come

to the fore in crises—perhaps family, altruism or leadership—often hold significance.

8. **Legacy Reflection:** Think about the legacy you want to leave behind. What three values do you want to be remembered for? What will people say they admired about you at your funeral?

9. **Consolidation:** Some values might be different words that hold similar meanings for you. See if any can be grouped under a single umbrella term. Ideally, your three values should be complimentary but not too similar. For example, if you value kindness and generosity, you could consolidate these as altruism.

For the brave amongst you, Brené Brown, in her work on vulnerability and courage, suggests that people should focus on only two core values. She believes that by narrowing it down, individuals will be even more clear about what matters. I think that three values offer more flexibility, protecting against being overly biased toward one or two specific values.

Rank Your Values

Now, before we finish up, I'd like you to rank your three values. While all three are fundamental, arranging them in a priority order ensures clarity during situations where values might conflict.

Consider this example:

As the last rays of sunset permeate the 18th floor of a glass office building, Maya, a dynamic HR leader, finds herself at a crossroads. Her values, in order of priority, are physical well-being, accomplishment, and respect. She's looking forward to her 7 p.m. Pilates class, a personal commitment she rarely misses. However, a last-minute email from the CEO requests her presence at an impromptu strategy session—at the same time as Pilates. If she misses Pilates, she will feel resentment towards her CEO and workplace. However, she would like to participate because she wants to advance her career. Physical well-being versus accomplishment. How does Maya decide?

Option A: Because physical well-being is Maya's top value, she can decisively yet politely decline the meeting. It's an easy decision. But does not attending threaten her at the level of survival? Would it compromise her job security? As mentioned earlier, survival values usually short-circuit our higher values-based behaviors—and for good reason. If Maya is confident that her role is secure, she may benefit from asserting clear boundaries with her CEO, demonstrating that she lives with integrity.

Option B: Maya realizes the importance of participating in company strategy, plus there is a risk that others will undermine her. So, she reframes the situation and sees it not as a loss of Pilates hour but as a testament to her dedication and adaptability. In this case, she decides to practice Pilates at home before the meeting. There are, after all, many great instructors on YouTube.

The purpose of having a values hierarchy is to enable cognitive flex-ibility, reducing resentment and regret in our lives. Resentment is a poison you create for someone else and then drink yourself. Engaging your three values gives you options for guiding—and reframing—how you will react or respond to challenges.

HOW TO RANK YOUR VALUES

Here is how to rank your top three values in order of personal impor-tance and potential impact.

Step 1: Deep-Dive Reflection

Conduct a deep-dive reflection for each of your three values. This means spending some time in a quiet place with paper, pen, and this book. Consider how each value manifests in your life, its importance to you, and specific instances where it has guided your decisions, behaviors, and overall sense of fulfillment.

Step 2: Impact and Fulfillment Assessment

Criteria: Assess each value based on its impact on your life and the fulfillment it brings. Use these questions to guide your assessment:

- **Impact:** How does prioritizing this value enrich my life and the lives of those around me?
- **Fulfillment:** How much genuine satisfaction and joy do I derive from living according to this value?

Step 3: Consistency and Resilience Check

Criteria: Evaluate each value for its consistency in your life and resilience to changes.

- **Consistency:** Has this value been a steady guide across different areas and phases of my life?
- **Resilience:** Is my commitment to this value strong, even when faced with challenges or changes in external circumstances?

Step 4: Comparative Analysis

Based on your reflections and assessments, compare each value against the others. Consider which value you would prioritize if you had to make a difficult choice that could only align with one of these values. If people said only one thing about you at your funeral, what would they say? For example, "Brad was kind." Does that describe you without the need for additional values? If so, it is your number one.

Step 5: Ranking Exercise

Based on the deep-dive reflections, impact and fulfillment assessment, consistency and resilience check, and comparative analysis, rank the values from 1 to 3, with 1 being the most important value to you personally.

Final Reflection

Reflect on your ranked values. Do they align with your authentic self? This final reflection is crucial to ensure the ranking genuinely reflects the essence of what is most important to you.

If you're stuck, I highly recommend using an AI tool like ChatGPT to help you brainstorm. Prompt it by writing: help me rank my top three values. My values are {list them}.

> **Action:** What are your top three values? Write them down in order of importance.

VALUES AS IDENTITY

Embracing values as integral parts of your identity is a powerful shift that can transform how you live your life.

Consider this: rather than simply valuing compassion as an item on your list, imagine saying, "I am a compassionate person" in the mirror every day. If you do this, you won't be just adopting compassion as a value—you'll weave it into the fabric of your identity. This subtle linguistic shift has profound implications for behavior. It's not about aiming to act compassionately; it is about being compassionate in every interaction.

Let's look at how you might apply this technique to your top three values:

1. **Integrity:** Instead of striving to act with integrity, affirm, "I am a person of integrity." This statement becomes a foundational truth about yourself, informing every decision and action you take.

2. **Courage:** Move beyond simply valuing bravery and declare, "I am a courageous person." This assertion empowers you to face challenges head-on, knowing that courage is an intrinsic part of who you are.

3. **Curiosity:** Instead of just valuing curiosity, say, "I am a curious person." This transforms every moment into an opportunity for learning and discovery, with curiosity as a driving force in your pursuit of knowledge.

By defining your values as core aspects of your identity, you create a self-fulfilling prophecy. This isn't just about setting behavioral goals; it's about crafting a personal narrative where your values become so deeply embedded in your sense of self that they become instinctive. It's a proactive approach to personal development, one where you live your values so authentically that they become synonymous with who you are.

Action: For each of your top three values, write a statement that embeds the value into your identity. The format is: I am a {value as an adjective} person.

THE SURVIVAL LAYER

You might be wondering why we've skipped the Survival layer of the Values Pyramid up to this point. It's a valid question. For some, the focus on survival aligns perfectly with their values, providing a deep sense of fulfillment. Think about people living in a war zone or in poverty. In these circumstances, survival will be the utmost priority. However, the essence of starting with values is to elevate our collective consciousness to shape a brighter future for all. That's why, for those willing and able to join this mission, we must strive to secure our safety, so that we can then learn, grow, help others, and create positive impact.

Of course, our survival instincts will kick in occasionally. When our fundamental needs are at risk, we naturally feel anxious, and our focus narrows. It is good to be aware of the survival values that emerge amid change, challenge, and uncertainty:

1. **Safety:** Being shielded from danger, risk, or injury.

2. **Nourishment:** Essential elements required for health and well-being, predominantly provided by food and water.

3. **Economic Stability:** The certainty of financial means that ensures a reliable income and opportunities for financial advancement.

4. **Well-being:** A harmonious state where one is healthy, comfortable, and content.

5. **Housing:** Having a secure and stable place to live.

6. **Protection:** Safeguarding against harm or damage.

7. **Consistency:** Maintaining a standard of performance without significant fluctuation.

8. **Energy Security:** Uninterrupted access to affordable and reliable energy sources.

9. **Recovery:** The journey back to a state of health, soundness, or vigor.

10. **Apparel:** Clothing designed for protection, comfort, or style.

11. **Sanitation:** The maintenance of clean conditions to promote health and prevent disease.

12. **Accessibility:** The ease with which resources can be reached or utilized.

Action: Are all of your survival values being met? Which areas are most at risk? Expressing gratitude for the fact that your survival values are satisfied is an important exercise that will improve your mental and physical well-being.

PSYCHEDELICS, PLANT MEDICINE AND VALUES

This section would not be complete without mentioning the power of plant medicines for introspection and self-discovery. A recent wave of interest has seen figures like Tim Ferriss and Professor Andrew Huberman openly discussing the therapeutic potential of psychedelics on their podcasts, and there is no shortage of content—even Netflix documentaries—about the risks and benefits. As academic studies demonstrate positive and sometimes astounding results for treating depression, PTSD, and addiction, people have started paying attention to the power of altered states of consciousness for profound insights and healing.

For thousands—perhaps hundreds of thousands—of years, cultures worldwide have used plant medicines in sacred rituals to deepen their connection to self, others, and the natural world. The Stoned Ape Theory, proposed by ethnobotanist Terence McKenna, goes as far as suggesting that the consumption of psychedelic substances, specifically psilocybin mushrooms, played a critical role in the evolutionary development of early human cognition and consciousness.

In my experience, plant medicines remove distracting layers of thought, enabling clear insight into what matters. I was at an ayahuasca ceremony many years ago—before such things were trendy—and in one of my visions, my grandfather handed me a tiny baby wrapped in a blue blanket. Looking down, I realized that the baby was me. I comforted that small child and told him everything was going to be okay. And it was. In another vision, I was writing books that would one day help people. Importantly, I was alerted to behaviors that were not aligned with my core values.

Some potential benefits of psychedelics include:

1. **Deepening Self-Awareness:** Psychedelics, when used in a controlled and supportive environment, can induce states of consciousness that allow individuals to see beyond their habitual thought patterns. This altered state can reveal deeply held values that might have been obscured by daily distractions or societal pressures.

2. **Confronting Traumas:** Traumatic experiences can distort our perception of self and the world around us. Psychedelics and plant medicines like ayahuasca and psilocybin mushrooms can help individuals confront and heal from these traumas, allowing them to realign with their core values.

3. **Connecting to the Collective:** Many users report a heightened sense of interconnectedness during their experiences, reinforcing values related to empathy, compassion, and community.

4. **Nature and Spirituality:** Plant medicines can cultivate a deep sense of connection to the natural world, emphasizing the value of nature stewardship and spiritual growth.

Embarking on a medicinal journey with the intent to discover your core values may unlock a profound and mystical experience. One study found that a single psilocybin trip was considered by participants to be among the most personally meaningful and spiritually significant experiences of their lives. This is not about partying; it is about deep contemplation with clear intention, including a plan to integrate insights into everyday life.

However, it's critical to approach the use of psychedelics and plant medicines with caution and respect. While they can offer transformative insights, they're not a panacea and are not suitable for everyone. Always consider set (mindset), setting (environment), and guidance (from experienced facilitators or therapists) when embarking on such journeys. Furthermore, always consider the legal status and potential health risks of any substance. Potential risks include psychological distress, adverse reactions, exacerbation of existing mental health conditions, interactions with other medications, and legal consequences.

Proper preparation and professional support are essential to ensure safety and maximize benefits.

BEWARE OF JUNK VALUES

Before we progress to the next section, it's time to perform a quick values audit. Whether we realize it or not, most of us have adopted at least a few "junk values," as prescribed by social media, convenience, and consumer culture. Signs that you possess junk values include chasing after material possessions with the belief that they'll bring happiness, comparing yourself to others on social media, experiencing anxiety over not living up to someone else's standards, or feeling the pressure to prioritize trends and prestige over personal well-being and genuine relationships. Regret is also a strong indicator that you have acted out of alignment with who you really are.

Junk values divert us from what truly matters, leading to a life driven by external validation (extrinsic values) rather than authenticity (intrinsic values). It's essential to recognize and address these junk values, replacing them with ones that genuinely resonate.

In his book *Lost Connections*, Johann Hari explores the concept of junk values, explaining that, much like junk food lacks the nutrients our bodies need, junk values lack the emotional and psychological sustenance required for our well-being. These are values that prioritize material success, social status, appearance, or the approval of others over more intrinsic values like meaningful relationships, personal growth, and contributing to the welfare of others.

The trouble with junk values is that they feed into a perpetual cycle of dissatisfaction. Just as consuming junk food leaves us hungry for more, junk values keep us on a treadmill of constant craving, pushing us to pursue things that don't bring long-term fulfillment. We may get a short burst of happiness from acquiring the latest smartphone, landing a high-paying job, or getting more likes on social media, but these feelings are transient. Once the initial buzz wears off, we are back at square one, if not worse.

Why worse? Because constantly chasing external validation or material possessions shifts our focus away from what genuinely enriches our lives. It creates a void that we try to fill with more of the same, perpetuating a cycle that ultimately leaves us feeling empty, disconnected, and, in many cases, depressed.

Johann Hari argues that this disconnection from meaningful values is one of the leading causes of the modern epidemic of depression and anxiety. To reclaim our mental health, he suggests that we must reorient our lives around more nourishing values—those that foster connection, purpose, and contentment.

Your junk values might surface when you are stressed or under high pressure. Despite valuing well-being, you might impulsively buy fast food and skip exercising. Or instead of practicing kindness, you might shout at the kids—and later regret it. Regret is a clear sign that a value has been violated. Pay close attention to this feeling.

Here are examples of some common junk values:

1. **Materialism:** Valuing possessions or wealth as primary success indicators.

2. **Fame:** Seeking widespread recognition as validation of self-worth.

3. **External Approval:** Relying on others' validation for self-esteem.

4. **Perfectionism:** Chasing unattainable perfection, leading to distress and dissatisfaction.

5. **Power Over Others:** Valuing control over others as success.

6. **Conformity:** Prioritizing societal norms over authentic self-expression.

7. **Instant Gratification:** Preferring immediate pleasure over long-term benefits.

8. **Competitiveness:** Viewing success as outdoing others, not personal growth.

9. **Status:** Seeking social prestige as a primary goal.

10. **Consumerism:** Believing happiness comes from constant consumption.

11. **Superficial Beauty:** Overvaluing physical appearance over inner qualities.

12. **Envy:** Desiring others' success or possessions, leading to resentment.

13. **Workaholism:** Prioritizing work over personal life and relationships.

14. **Narcissism:** Focusing excessively on oneself at the expense of empathy for others.

15. **Cynicism:** Distrusting or disparaging the motives of others, hindering genuine connections.

16. **Passivity:** Avoiding action or decision-making, leading to a lack of control over one's life.

17. **Short-Term Thinking:** Focusing on the immediate future at the expense of long-term planning and goals.

18. **Indifference to Learning:** Valuing ignorance or a lack of curiosity about the world.

19. **Overindulgence:** Pursuing excessive pleasures or luxuries to the detriment of health or well-being.

20. **Change Aversion:** Resisting change or growth, leading to stagnation.

21. **Fast Food:** Valuing convenience and immediate satisfaction over nutritional quality and the benefits of more mindful eating.

22. **Snacking:** Choosing temporary pleasure despite the weight gain and health implications.

23. **Alcohol:** Overindulging in substances to provide a temporary relief from suffering or boredom.

24. **Victimhood:** Holding onto a mentality where one consistently sees themselves as the victim in various situations.

25. **FOBO (Fear Of Being Offline):** Valuing constant connectivity to the extent that it detrimentally affects presence, focus, and mental wellbeing.

26. **FOMO (Fear Of Missing Out):** The desire to be included in an endless stream of social activities and trends, driven by the fear of being left out.

Shifting Away from Junk Values

Replacing a behavior that contradicts your core values with one that aligns with them is a journey of self-awareness and habit reformation. If well-being is a core value and you find yourself reaching for fast food, pause and ask yourself what is driving this choice. Is it convenience? Hunger? Emotional comfort?

Once the trigger is identified, you need to have a pre-planned response that diffuses the intensity of emotions (such as craving) associated with the junk value, ideally injecting a behavior associated with one of your core values. If well-being is your priority, your response could be having healthy snacks readily available or choosing a restaurant that offers nutritious options. This strategy, known as 'if-then' planning in behavioral psychology, is about creating a plan for when you encounter a situation that triggers a junk value.

How to Create an 'If-Then' Plan

The process involves several steps:

1. **Awareness:** Consciously recognize when you're about to engage in a behavior driven by a junk value.

2. **Pause and Reflect:** Give yourself a moment to consider the consequences of your action and how it diverges from a core value. For example, consider how reaching for that sugary energy drink contradicts your value of well-being. When in doubt, breathe out. Between stimulus and response there is a space, and in that space lies your freedom to choose.

3. **Redirect:** Leverage the 'if-then' plan. If you're about to eat fast food, then you have an opportunity to choose the pre-prepared healthier option instead. Ask yourself, "Which choice will make the future version of me proud?"

4. **Reinforce:** Celebrate the small victories when you successfully align your actions with your values. This positive reinforcement makes the new behavior more appealing.

5. **Repeat:** Habits are formed through repetition. The more you choose the action that aligns with your core value, the more it becomes a part of your routine and identity.

6. **Resilience:** If you falter, treat it as a learning experience, not a failure. Resilience is key in the process of change.

Remember, it's not about perfection; it's about progress. Each choice that aligns with your values is a step towards fulfillment.

> **Action:** When do you experience regret? For example, perhaps after wasting hours crafting an Instagram post, eating unhealthy food, or skipping a gym day. In these examples, the junk values might be the need for external validation, convenience, and avoiding discomfort, respectively. What are your junk values and how do they contrast with your core values? Can you construct an 'if-then' plan for unwanted behaviors that are driven by junk values?

4

LIVE YOUR VALUES

JOSEPH CAMPBELL, THE celebrated mythologist, introduced the world to the hero's journey—a universal narrative framework that captures the essence of human transformation and can be found across stories, scriptures, myths, and cultures. The framework consists of a cyclical sequence: the hero ventures from the known to the unknown, confronts challenges and temptations, gains wisdom or abilities, and eventually returns home transformed. While Campbell's hero's journey framework has been dissected from various angles, one aspect that often goes understated is the role of core values in guiding this transformational odyssey.

At the outset of the journey, the hero is often driven by values which he may not fully comprehend. As he ventures into the unknown, crossing the threshold between his old life and the new adventure, these values are tested and refined. A series of trials, mentors, and betrayals challenge the hero's resolve, but they activate his values, doing what is right even when it causes suffering. Whether it's Neo's value of justice and revenge after taking the red pill in *The Matrix* or Frodo Baggins' loyalty and responsibility in *The Lord of the Rings*, the hero's values guide him through these challenges.

These values don't merely help the hero conquer foes or find treasures; they also help him confront and resolve his inner conflicts. This is where the real transformation occurs. The return journey, often laden with more challenges, brings the hero back to his starting point, but he is no longer the same person he was at the beginning.

He brings back something greater—an elixir of wisdom, perhaps, or a treasure—but most importantly, he brings a renewed and deepened understanding of his core values. The ripple effect of sharing his story is that others appreciate and perhaps adopt the same values that supported the hero's success.

In essence, the hero's journey, as conceived by Campbell, is not just an external adventure but a voyage of self-discovery and personal alignment. It's a framework that sheds light on how our values are forged, tested, and ultimately affirmed, providing each of us with the potential for heroic transformation in our lives.

Let's consider a work of literature—and a blockbuster television series—that is teeming with examples of misaligned and conflicting values. In the sprawling epic, *Game of Thrones*, every character is on a hero's journey, guided by a distinct set of values that drives his or her actions, alliances, and ultimate destiny. Take Jon Snow, for example, who values honor and duty above all else. Despite treacherous political landscapes and existential threats, his unwavering commitment to these values earns him loyalty and respect but also sparks complex moral dilemmas.

At the other end of the spectrum is Daenerys Targaryen. Her values of social justice, freedom, and ambition shaped her journey from a powerless exile to a formidable conqueror. Her arc is a riveting example of how values evolve, as her initial commitment to liberation becomes increasingly tarnished by the complexities of power and governance.

Or consider Tyrion Lannister, whose values of intellect, pragmatism, and humor help him navigate the perilous terrain of Westeros politics. He uses his wits not just for survival but to exert influence in a world that often discriminates against him. Tyrion's journey exemplifies how holding true to one's values can bring both triumph and hardship.

Even antagonists like Cersei Lannister have their own hero's journey, driven by core values such as family, legacy, and power. These values happen to conflict with those of other characters, but in her narrative, they serve as her guiding light and ultimate downfall.

In *Game of Thrones*, each character's journey becomes a nuanced exploration of how values not only guide us but also define us. They are heroes and anti-heroes in their own epics, striving and failing, conquering and being vanquished, all while their values shape their paths in complex, often tragic, ways.

Have you ever wondered why certain historical and contemporary figures evoke such strong emotions, be it admiration or aversion? The answer often lies in their core values. When someone's values align closely with our own, we are more likely to admire and respect that person, regardless of the scale or nature of their achievements. Conversely, when their values clash with ours, admiration can quickly turn into disapproval.

Take Mahatma Gandhi, for instance. His values of non-violence, humility, and social justice resonate with people across the world, making him a universal symbol of peaceful resistance. Or consider Martin Luther King Jr., whose commitment to equality and civil rights has cemented his legacy as one of the most admired figures in modern history. Similarly, ancient figures like Socrates, who valued wisdom and intellectual rigor, and religious leaders like Jesus Christ and the Buddha, who preached love, compassion, and enlightenment, have left an indelible mark on humanity.

But values can also divide us. Controversial figures like Napoleon Bonaparte or Fidel Castro elicit mixed feelings, not merely because of their actions but also because of the values those actions represent. Napoleon, for example, stood for social mobility and secular governance but was also an imperialist at heart, making him a divisive character depending on the varied values of contemporary observers and historical commentators.

Even in our daily lives, we often find ourselves naturally drawn to or repelled by people based on how well their core values align with ours. So, the next time you find yourself admiring or disliking someone, ask yourself: Is it their achievements that you're responding to, or is it their core values? Chances are, it's the latter that stirs your soul.

FROM VALUES TO MICRO-HABITS

A few years ago, I facilitated a workshop for a group of business owners in New Zealand. One attendee, who we'll name Mike, was noticeably unwell, puffing heavily, his mobility compromised by excess weight. During our discussion on micro-habits, I encouraged everyone to pinpoint a small, health-related change they could repeat on a daily basis. Mike, with a tone of defeat, declared that he'd never be fit again. Curious, I inquired if he'd ever been fit. He revealed that he used to be a bodybuilder.

His favorite exercise? "Bench press," he responded without hesitation.

After some light-hearted banter about skipping the infamous 'leg day,' I posed another question: "What's a daily habit you never miss?" Mike mentioned making coffee every morning at 7 a.m.

I asked how many pushups he could manage right now. "About five," he said. I then asked, "How about doing those five pushups while your coffee brews every morning at 7 a.m.?" He gave a noncommittal shrug, and we moved on.

Years later, an acquaintance updated me on Mike's journey. Remarkably, Mike had embraced the pushup challenge. He began with five pushups daily while his coffee brewed, amounting to 1,825 pushups in the first year—pushups he wouldn't have otherwise done. Inspired by his progress, he upped the count to 10 daily pushups the following year, totaling 3,650 by year's end. This small yet consistent routine paved the way for more. He added a minute of stretching followed by five minutes of meditation. Three years later, Mike had not only regained his physique but also enjoyed a rejuvenated mindset, and he now shares his transformative journey at various events.

What *Are* Micro-Habits Anyway?

At the core, micro-habits are incremental actions, so minuscule that they might seem trivial at a glance. However, when repeated consistently, these small actions build upon each other, culminating in profound behavioral shifts over time.

James Clear and BJ Fogg, prominent figures in the realm of behavioral change, have promoted the power of micro-habits in their bestselling books. Clear, in *Atomic Habits,* explains how minor changes, when compounded, lead to remarkable results. Fogg's *Tiny Habits* emphasizes how small, easily achievable behaviors appended to existing routines and celebrated with positive reinforcement lead to lasting habit formation.

So, where does the "values-based" aspect of micro-habits come into play? When micro-habits are crafted to resonate with our core values, they propel us toward fulfillment one small step at a time. Each time we engage in a values-based micro-habit, it's like making a statement: "This is who I am, and this is what I stand for." It's not just about the act itself but the profound meaning behind it.

Values-based micro-habits, therefore, harness the dual power of the simplicity of micro-actions and the deep resonance of core values. They're not just habits; they're reflections of our identity. When our daily routines echo our values, the alignment fosters what we might call micro-fulfillment (you heard that here first), amplifying the efficacy of the habits and triggering a virtuous cycle of behavioral reinforcement.

Why Micro-Habits Bypass Resistance to Change

The human body and mind are wired for equilibrium. From our body temperature to blood sugar levels, numerous mechanisms work diligently to maintain a steady state called homeostasis. This innate drive towards balance isn't restricted to our physical selves; it extends to our behaviors, habits, and even our thoughts.

Homeostasis and Resistance to Change

Homeostasis is the body's natural inclination to maintain internal stability in response to external changes. For instance, when our body temperature rises, we sweat to cool down; when it drops, we shiver to produce heat.

Behaviorally, homeostasis can be seen in our resistance to change. Our brains have evolved to conserve energy, meaning they're wired to follow the path of least resistance. When we try to adopt a new habit, especially a drastic one, our brain perceives it as an energy-consuming anomaly, setting off alarm bells. This resistance is our mind's attempt to maintain behavioral homeostasis, much like our body's effort to maintain a stable temperature.

How Micro-Habits Bypass This Resistance

Micro-habits, given their "micro" nature, are sneaky. They're so small and seemingly insignificant that our brain doesn't register them as threats to our established routines or physiological energy conservation goals. By being diminutive,

- **They Reduce Fear:** Large changes can be intimidating and provoke anxiety, making us more likely to avoid or postpone them. In contrast, a tiny change—like doing two minutes of meditation or writing one sentence of a report—seems doable and non-threatening.

- **They Minimize Effort:** Our brains are less likely to resist actions that require minimal effort. Starting with a 5-minute walk instead of an hour-long workout is more approachable, and it sidesteps the brain's energy-saving objections.
- **They Build Consistency:** Since micro-habits are easier to execute, they can be practiced more consistently. Over time, this consistent practice reprograms our brain, establishing the micro-habit as a new norm, gradually shifting our behavioral homeostasis.

By creatively and intelligently leveraging micro-habits, we're essentially using a psychological backdoor, circumventing the brain's resistance to change. When these habits compound over time, as Clear notes in *Atomic Habits*, we find that we've made significant changes without the monumental initial effort or the daunting prospect of a significant life overhaul.

1 Percent Better Every Day

Clear's *Atomic Habit*s is not just about building habits; it's about creating systems that foster consistent growth and change.

Imagine improving by just 1% every day. On its own, this tiny increment might seem negligible, almost invisible in the short run. However, when applied consistently over a longer period, the cumulative effect is staggering.

Mathematically, this can be represented as:

$$1.01^{365} \approx 37.78$$

This means that if you were to improve by just 1% every day for a year, you'd be more than 37 times better by the end of the year.

This principle isn't only applicable to building positive habits. If you were to decline by 1% every day, you'd reduce to virtually zero by the end of the year. Mathematically:

$$0.99^{365} \approx 0.03$$

It's clear that, while positive habits compound to provide exponential benefits, negative habits can drag you down at an equally rapid pace.

But why is being 1% better each day significant in the context of habits?

1. **Long-Term Vision:** It reinforces the idea that true change takes time. Rather than getting disheartened by the lack of immediate transformation, we should focus on consistent progress.

2. **Motivation through Small Wins:** Recognizing the 1% improvement helps in celebrating the small victories, which can serve as motivation to continue the habit.

3. **A Shift in Perspective:** It allows individuals to realize that success isn't born from overnight changes but from the small, consistent efforts made every day.

The philosophy underlying the 37x improvement is an ode to patience, perseverance, and the incredible power of compound growth. By making tiny positive changes every day, one can achieve results that seem almost unfathomable in the long run. Refer back to Mike's story for an example of real-world transformation.

How to Set Values-Based Micro-Habits

Now, let's get practical. It's time to bring your values to life through deliberately applied practice. Follow this process:

1. **Pick a Core Value:** You have your list of three. Which value would you like to embed in your daily activity? For this example, let's choose "kindness."

2. **Start Small:** Choose a micro-habit that aligns with your core value. The habit should be simple enough to be done daily with minimal resistance. For "kindness," a micro-habit could be giving a genuine compliment to one person each day.

3. **Anchor the Micro-Habit:** Attach your new micro-habit to an existing habit or routine. If you already have a habit of morning coffee, you could compliment someone during that coffee break. If no-one is around, send a text message or email.

4. **Make It Attractive:** Make the micro-habit appealing. This can mean setting reminders with encouraging messages or rewarding yourself after a week of consistent practice.

5. **Make It Easy:** Reduce friction to ensure your micro-habit is easily executable. For the habit of kindness, you could prepare some compliments in advance, or bring your phone so you can quickly send a message.

6. **Make It Satisfying:** Offer yourself immediate feedback or rewards. Marking an 'X' on a calendar or noting how the compliment made someone's day can serve as reinforcement.

7. **Track and Reflect:** At the end of each week, assess your consistency and the impact of the micro-habit on embodying your core value. Adjust if necessary.

8. **Scale Up Gradually:** Once the micro-habit becomes an integral part of your daily routine, consider amplifying it. Maybe you progress from one compliment to two, or perhaps you expand the gesture of kindness.

9. **Stay Aligned:** Regularly ensure that your micro-habit aligns with your core value. As you evolve, your values may shift, and so should your habits.

10. **Spread the Word:** Share your journey with friends, family, or colleagues. Encouraging others to adopt values-based micro-habits can create a ripple effect of positive change.

Examples of values-based micro-habits include:

- **Well-being:** Drink a glass of water immediately after waking up.
- **Continuous Learning:** Read a passage from an educational book after breakfast for 5 minutes every day.
- **Environmental Stewardship:** Pack a reusable water bottle and shopping bag before leaving the house.
- **Presence:** Engage in a 2-minute meditation session before logging into your computer at work.
- **Gratitude:** Write down one thing you're grateful for right before turning off your bedside lamp every night.

> **Action:** Select one of your values and turn it into a micro-habit. Use your values-based identity as a motivator. A statement like "I am a grateful person; therefore, I practice gratitude for one minute after dinner," gives depth and gravity to the micro-habit. Be sure to attach the new habit to one that is already reliably consistent. Track progress and insert new micro-habits as you gather momentum.

VALUES UNDER PRESSURE

Welcome to what might be the most useful part of this book. These principles have helped tens of thousands of people who have attended my workshops and seminars.

Under pressure, our values become obscured by the physical and mental fog of our stress response. This is because when we encounter stressors, our nervous system shifts into survival mode. Our system can handle stress in acute bursts, but when it becomes chronic, this can not only derail our values but can also lead to adverse health outcomes in the form of inflammation, heart attacks, and strokes.

Stress can also become a habit. In fact, some people unwittingly begin to value the feeling of being stressed (talk about a junk value!). Workaholism, for example, is often driven by a chemical cocktail of stress hormones that cause hyperarousal and an inability to switch off. I've spoken to many senior executives who say they actually feel stressed when they're not stressed—because stress has become part of their identity and daily routine.

The point is to be aware that activating our body's stress response means that immediate reactions are no longer deliberate, but instead are reflexes shaped by our nervous system's survival instincts. This habitual behavior can eclipse values-driven behavior, making it challenging to act in ways that align with what matters most. If you're not thriving or feeling engaged though all of your basic life needs are met, chances are you're experiencing high levels of stress.

Now, I invite you to sit back and join me for one of my favorite experiences in the world: a game safari. I'm using my best David Attenborough narration for the next part. Use your imagination to follow along attentively.

On a vast, sun-drenched expanse of the African savannah, a solitary zebra grazes, its stripes shimmering under the golden glow. The scene exudes a sense of calm; the world seems still, save for the gentle rustling of grass.

But, unbeknownst to our striped protagonist, danger lurks nearby. Hidden amidst the tall golden grasses, a lion—a master of stealth— watches intently. As the wind shifts, alerting the zebra to impending peril, tension fills the air. The stillness is shattered as the lion erupts into a ferocious sprint, launching its assault.

The zebra, powered by instinct, immediately bolts. The peaceful savannah transforms into a high-speed chase scene. The zebra's agility shines as it dodges and weaves, avoiding the lion's lethal claws. Each stride is a testament to nature's raw power and the primal dance of predator and prey.

Minutes feel like hours, but the lion's energy starts to wane. Realizing its meal will escape today, the predator slows, eventually halting, while the zebra, sensing the reprieve, slows its pace, moving towards a familiar watering hole.

Eager to recuperate, the zebra bends down, taking long, satisfying gulps from the refreshing pool. Each sip not only replenishes its spent body but also aids in flushing out the accumulated stress hormones. As it drinks, its muscles, recently tense with adrenaline, begin to relax, and the rhythmic sounds of the watering hole further calm its nerves.

Having navigated the raw intensity of life and death and finding safety once again, the zebra returns to grazing peacefully as the sun continues its descent, casting long shadows across the vast grasslands.

The zebra, in this example, succeeded in aligning its behaviors with the value of self-preservation. Here's the neurophysiology of what happened:

- **Immediate Hormonal Surge:** The moment the zebra perceives danger, its brain's amygdala—a region responsible for processing threats—sends an emergency signal to the hypothalamus. This is the command center for the "fight or flight" response. The hypothalamus triggers the adrenal glands, situated atop the kidneys, to release a surge of adrenaline (also known as epinephrine).
- **Physiological Turbo Boost:** Adrenaline prepares the zebra for rapid action. Its heart rate skyrockets, pumping blood faster to the leg muscles. The bronchi in the lungs dilate, allowing for

increased oxygen intake. The pupils enlarge for better visual acuity. Energy stores are mobilized, flooding the bloodstream with glucose for quick energy.

- **Slowing Non-Essentials:** Processes not immediately essential for escape are dialed down. Digestion slows; after all, processing food isn't a priority when running for one's life. Growth, reproduction, and immune responses take a backseat.
- **Cortisol's Role:** A bit later in this response cascade, the adrenal glands release cortisol, another stress hormone. While adrenaline deals with the immediate response, cortisol helps marshal systems for prolonged action and modulates energy supplies.
- **Post Danger Reset:** When the zebra evades the lion, the parasympathetic nervous system starts the process of calming the body down. The stress hormones decrease, heart rate slows, and regular bodily functions like digestion gradually resume. The zebra goes back to grazing, the traumatic event seemingly forgotten.

This rapid, full-body response is beautifully efficient for life-or-death situations in the wild.

Let's explore what happens to another animal. One that inhabits a glass-windowed building in the center of what humans call "a city."

Deep within the maze of an open-plan office, John sits at his desk, immersed in the rhythmic tapping of keys and the soft hum of overhead fluorescent lights. His wife and daughter stare at him from a photograph pinned to the divider that separates him from a colleague. The atmosphere is one of subdued concentration, a world of deadlines, projects, and coffee.

But in this ecosystem, just like in the savannah, unexpected dangers can lurk. An email pops up on John's screen, an invitation from his boss for an impromptu meeting. A flutter of unease stirs in John's chest. The suddenness of the invite, the lack of an agenda—these are the warning signs like a subtle shift in the wind.

As John walks to the meeting room, he can feel his heart rate quicken, mirroring our zebra's initial surge of adrenaline. Each step is heavy, echoing the zebra's desperate gallop. Inside, his boss, a figure of authority and influence, sits waiting, not unlike a lion on the savannah. The ensuing conversation feels like a chase, a dance of questions, answers, and subtle power plays.

The meeting ends, not with a roar, but with a seemingly benign "We'll need to discuss this further." John, much like the zebra post-chase, retreats to the sanctuary of his desk. But here's where their paths diverge.

Instead of drinking from a peaceful watering hole and slowly letting go of the stress, John begins to ruminate. The encounter plays over and over in his mind—every word, every nuance, every possible implication. Each replay injects another dose of stress hormones into his system.

As the day stretches into evening, the mental replays don't relent. At home, instead of seeking comfort from family, John withdraws, isolating himself. The tranquility of night doesn't grant him the rest he needs. His mind, stuck in overdrive, keeps him tossing and turning. This cycle, unchecked, starts to erode his mental well-being. Over time, the momentary stressful event casts a long, shadowy haze over his life, pushing him to the precipice of a quiet, insidious depression.

Let's quickly deconstruct what happened in John's body as the event unfolded.

Inside John's body, as he reads the email from his boss, there's an immediate physiological response. His autonomic nervous system, the system responsible for involuntary bodily functions, shifts into high gear. The sympathetic branch—responsible for fight and flight—is activated. His adrenal glands release a cocktail of stress hormones, primarily adrenaline and cortisol. John's heart rate and blood pressure increase, and his senses sharpen.

As he walks to the meeting room, his palms might become sweaty, a side effect of the adrenaline preparing his body for quick action. His pupils dilate, allowing in more light so he can assess the situation better. Blood is redirected to major muscle groups, getting them ready for rapid movement. His breathing becomes shallower as the body tries to take in more oxygen in preparation for what's next.

Inside the meeting room, his body remains in this heightened state. Cortisol in particular plays a role in ensuring that energy is readily available by increasing glucose in the bloodstream. It also suppresses non-essential functions like digestion, which is why stress can often cause an upset stomach or lack of appetite.

Then, after the meeting, when he should ideally transition to a rest-and-digest state activated by the parasympathetic nervous system, rumination—in the form of repetitive thoughts—keeps his cortisol levels elevated.

At home, his body struggles to transition to a more restful state. Elevated cortisol levels at night are particularly problematic as they interfere with the natural circadian rhythm and inhibit the production of melatonin, the hormone responsible for sleep.

Chronic activation of this stress response, especially when there's no physical outlet like running (as the zebra did) or a counterbalancing relaxation response, can lead to a host of health issues, including sleep problems, a weakened immune system, anxiety, and depression.

The zebra's experience with stress is acute; it's intense but short-lived. For John, the stress becomes chronic. When a lion approaches, the zebra doesn't ruminate or wonder about the lion's intentions. There's no analysis or introspection; there's just a pure, unadulterated, and immediate response. The zebra's nervous system propels it into swift action—either to fight briefly or, more likely, to flee. This response, honed over millennia, is a beautifully effective mechanism for an environment where physical threats are the primary concern.

However, humans, particularly in our modern era, don't fit neatly into this ancient biological script. Our ancestors experienced stressors not unlike the zebra's: predators, environmental dangers, and intertribal conflicts. Thus, our bodies evolved to deal with acute, immediate threats, responding with a surge of stress hormones that would fuel either a rapid escape or a physical confrontation.

Fast forward to today, and our stressors look dramatically different. They're more often psychological than physical: a looming deadline, a tense relationship, financial worries, or an unexpected email from a boss. Yet our bodies react as if these modern stressors are lions lurking in the grass, triggering the same old fight-or-flight response. The problem is that this response isn't well-suited for our modern challenges. There's no lion to run from; there's just an uncomfortable email. There's no immediate physical threat, just a vague, looming sense of unease about tomorrow.

Our evolutionary toolkit, while incredibly effective for survival in the wild, doesn't cater especially well to the nuances of modern living. This misalignment results in chronic stress, anxiety, and a host of associated health issues, leading to conditions like the vaguely defined but widely recognized "burnout."

A modern human's rush of adrenaline and cortisol doesn't have an outlet when the threat is a disapproving look or a challenging work email. Instead of being used to fuel a sprint or a fight, these chemicals linger in our system, causing dis-ease.

Recognizing this mismatch is the first step. Understanding that our stress response is an outdated tool in many of today's scenarios can empower us to seek better, more adaptive tools. We need skills to intentionally relax and regulate our emotions, to discern between actual threats and perceived ones, and to navigate a world that's far more complex than the binary life-or-death situations which our ancestors faced.

This is not merely for the sake of mental health, but it is, in fact, the cornerstone of aligning ourselves with our core values. But why is this ability to calm oneself so intricately linked to values alignment?

When our system is flooded with stress hormones, and we're stuck in a heightened state of alertness, our perspective narrows. Our brain's immediate priority is to survive. We're in a reactive mode, propelled by instincts. Our ability to contemplate, reflect, and align with broader, higher-level values diminishes. We become confined to the base level of the Values Pyramid, focused solely on securing survival.

However, by mastering the art of returning to a calm state, we clear the fog of primal fight-flight-or-freeze responses. We free up cognitive and emotional resources to reflect upon and embody higher-level values while reducing the chance that we will regret potentially destructive behaviors like shouting, crying, or outbursts. From a place of calm, we can more easily access values related to belonging, growth, impact, and fulfillment.

The challenge, then, becomes: How can we mitigate knee-jerk reactions—driven by the amygdala part of the brain—and deliberately calm our nervous system in the face of modern-day stressors?

You've come to the right place.

PRACTICAL TOOLS TO CULTIVATE CALM

- **Mindfulness Meditation:** Regular practice can reduce the reactivity of the amygdala, which serves as the brain's primary "alarm" center, and strengthen the prefrontal cortex's ability to regulate emotions. See page 89 for an example meditation.
- **Breathing:** Slowing and deepening your breath activates the parasympathetic nervous system, promoting a state of calm.

Techniques like the Resilience Institute's Tactical Calm (inhale for 4 seconds, exhale for 6) are particularly effective.

- **Progressive Muscle Relaxation:** Consciously tensing and then relaxing different muscle groups in the body can reduce physical tension and promote relaxation. Search for "Yoga Nidra" on YouTube for guided sessions.
- **Grounding Techniques:** Techniques like the "5-4-3-2-1" method (identify five things you can see, four you can touch, three you can hear, two you can smell, and one you can taste) can help reconnect you with the present moment.
- **Visualization:** Imagining a calm, safe place or scenario can help shift your emotional state.
- **Avoiding Stimulants:** Reducing or eliminating the intake of stimulants like caffeine can decrease overall nervous system arousal.
- **Regular Physical Activity:** Regular exercise can help metabolize stress hormones and activate the release of endorphins, nature's mood enhancers.

By engaging these tools and strategies to regain calm, we empower ourselves not just to respond more effectively to immediate stressors but also to elevate our actions and decisions, aligning them more closely with our higher-level values.

Note: When John eventually did reconnect with his boss, it turned out that there was no underlying issue. His boss simply wanted to catch-up. As Mark Twain said, "I've had a lot of worries in my life, most of which never happened."

Imagine if John had used one of the above techniques to calm his nervous system before, during, and especially after the interaction with his boss. His top core value is creativity and—from a calm state—he would have been able to navigate the meeting with his usual curious and creative mind. He also could have saved himself from several sleepless nights.

> **Action:** What is a situation in which you generally find yourself experiencing a fight (anger, frustration, hostility) or flight (fear, anxiety, worry) response? How does this impact your core values? Which value does it lead you to neglect? Can you practice calming yourself before, during, or after the next challenge?

VALUES-BASED DECISION MAKING

In Pietermaritzburg, South Africa, a young Dr. Imtiaz Sooliman was earning a reputation as a dedicated and skilled physician. While generally content, he had a persistent, nagging feeling that there was something more, something deeper he could offer the world.

On a journey to Istanbul, Dr. Sooliman found himself in the company of a wise Sufi teacher. The encounter was anything but ordinary. The Sufi's profound guidance, "Serve humanity unconditionally," resonated deeply with Sooliman. It was as if a veil had been lifted, connecting his value of service and his medical expertise to a broader mission.

Upon his return to South Africa, Dr. Sooliman viewed his profession in a new light. It wasn't just about treating ailments; it was about holistic healing, addressing not just physical wounds but societal ones. And so, the Gift of the Givers Foundation took shape, becoming the largest non-governmental disaster response organization of African origin. While its humanitarian achievements are celebrated today, the core remains the same—a mission born from a purpose beyond the self.

Dr. Sooliman was able to leverage the power of values to redefine his role as a physician. By making decisions through the lens of service, he expanded his impact far beyond the walls of a clinic.

RISKS TO DECISION MAKING

Before we dive into the methodology for making values-based decisions, we should be aware of certain hazards that can hinder clear and confident decision-making.

Analysis Paralysis

For the same reason that I recommend having just a few core values, I would suggest limiting your options whenever possible. The sheer weight of too many choices in life can lead to analysis paralysis. Think about our modern world: with information at our fingertips and an overflowing abundance of available products, services, and even romantic partners, you'd assume that decisions would be easier than ever. Yet, ironically, this overflow often complicates our ability to choose.

The real drawback? Analysis paralysis triggers a freeze response. The moments we spend dissecting every detail are moments not spent moving forward. Not only does this waste precious time, but it also breeds stress, chips away at our self-confidence, and can even cost us opportunities. Remember, every choice, even a misstep, carves our path, teaching us something new about ourselves. Constant indecision can cause us to lose valuable life lessons while wearing thin the patience of those around us, affecting our personal and professional relationships.

But there's hope in the form of values-based decision-making. It's like cutting through the noise, focusing only on options that resonate with who you are and where you want to be.

People Pleasing

At the heart of people-pleasing lies a seemingly benign or even admirable intent: the pursuit of harmony. Yet, feeling compelled to always put others' needs above our own for approval or to dodge conflict can silently corrode our sense of self. It's a behavior that can unwittingly sabotage our decisions, happiness, and ultimate fulfillment. For those caught in this loop, decision-making becomes less about what resonates with them and more about others' expectations. It's like wearing a mask so often that you forget your own face. People pleasers make choices with the aim of winning smiles or nods of approval, losing sight of their values and dreams along the way. This chameleon-like existence can be draining, compromising self-esteem and stirring up quiet resentment.

Consider standing at life's crossroads: one path winds towards a job that speaks to your soul but is modest in pay; the other leads to a lucrative role that feels hollow but would earn you rounds of applause at family dinners. The people pleaser would gravitate towards the latter, trading their joy for fleeting applause, betraying their own values in the process.

Succumbing to the siren call of pleasing others is like building a house on sand—it might stand for a while, but it's far from stable. Decisions made under this influence often yield a harvest of discontent.

In stark contrast, when you root your choices in your own values, there's a profound alignment that comes into play. This alignment is the cornerstone of genuine satisfaction and joy that no amount of external praise can match. It gives you permission to break free from the exhausting performance of living up to every expectation but your own—and to embrace the authenticity of being you.

If you ever find yourself dancing to the rhythm of others' desires, pause. Ask yourself: Who's writing the story of my life? Reclaiming the pen might just be the first step to living a life that's undeniably yours.

OTHER RISKS TO DECISION-MAKING

There are many other potential risks to effective decision-making, including:

Emotional State: Strong emotions like anger, sadness, fear, or craving can cloud thought and lead to impulsive decisions that you might regret later. You might like to review the zebra story above to see how our default stress response sabotages values-aligned action.

Overconfidence: Overestimating your abilities or the accuracy of information can lead to risky decisions without adequately considering the consequences.

Cognitive Biases: Certain thinking patterns can distort our perception, leading us away from objective reasoning and values-aligned actions. Confirmation bias, for example, inclines us to favor information that corroborates our existing beliefs, potentially blinding us to alternatives that might be more aligned with our core values. Anchoring, another such bias, is the tendency to fix our judgments around initial information, which can inhibit our ability to make decisions that genuinely reflect our values. The availability heuristic is a mental shortcut that happens when we judge the likelihood of something based on how quickly examples come to mind. For instance, if we can easily remember news stories about shark attacks, we might wrongly think that shark attacks are more common than they really are. This can lead us to make choices out of fear, rather than based on what's really best for us or the community.

By understanding and mitigating the influence of cognitive biases, we can more effectively align our choices with our core values, ensuring that our actions contribute to a life that is not just reactive to biases but reflective of our deepest commitments to ourselves. For a more comprehensive guide on how cognitive biases impact values-based decision making, explore further at startwithvalues.com/cognitive-bias-values.

Fear of Failure: This can lead to risk-averse behavior, limiting opportunities for growth and achievement. It might also result in avoiding making a decision altogether.

Social Pressure: Aside from people pleasing, the broader influence of societal norms, cultural practices, or peer pressure can steer an individual away from making decisions based on their core values.

Short-Term Focus: The tendency to seek immediate gratification can overshadow long-term benefits, often leading to choices that don't serve one's broader goals or values.

Decision Fatigue: Making too many decisions in a short period can deplete one's mental energy, reducing the quality of choices made thereafter.

Sunk Cost Fallacy: The more we invest in something (time, money, effort), the harder it becomes to abandon it, even when continuing is not the best option. This can lead to poor future decisions that are made in an effort to justify or 'redeem' the original decision.

Inertia: Sometimes a fear of change or the comfort of the status quo can be so overpowering that it paralyzes the decision-making process, even when change may be necessary.

Uncertainty and Complexity: Some decisions have so many variables that it's difficult to predict outcomes accurately, which can make the decision-making process more difficult.

Ethical or Moral Conflicts: Sometimes we are caught between multiple choices that all have ethical implications, complicating the decision-making process.

USE INTUITION AS A GUIDE

Intuition—or "gut feel"—involves a mix of learned experience and innate biological processes, and is a subject of ongoing research. The phenomenon encompasses both emotion-based and cognitive processes, which is why intuition is more than just a feeling or a thought—it can be a powerful full-body experience. The brain is very good at recognizing patterns, even if they are complex and subtle. Over time, it compiles this data into a sort of knowledge base that it can draw from instantly. When a situation arises that calls upon this repository of subconscious information, the brain may provide an answer in what feels like a 'gut reaction' before the conscious mind has time to process the same information.

Taking this further, we arrive at the concept of "emotional tagging," which is part of the somatic marker hypothesis. When we act in alignment with our core values, we usually experience a sense of ease, satisfaction, or even joy. These positive emotions are not merely passing states; they become etched into our neural pathways as somatic markers, according to the theory proposed by leading neuroscientist and author Antonio Damasio. These markers are like visceral bookmarks, reminding us of the outcomes that resonated with our values. Over time, these emotional responses accumulate and create a somatic landscape that our subconscious taps into when we're faced with choices. This means that when a decision aligns with these positively marked experiences, we feel a compelling pull—a gut instinct—that guides us toward the choices that align with our values, reinforcing a virtuous cycle of value-led living.

Damasio's hypothesis illuminates the profound and complicated dance between emotion and cognition. Rather than being at odds, they collaborate: our emotions point a spotlight on the paths most likely to fulfill us, guiding us through life's maze with the wisdom of our past experiences. These somatic markers operate beneath the surface of our conscious mind, subtly influencing the decision-making process. On the flip side, negative somatic markers serve as an internal alarm system, guiding us away from potential threats and undesirable outcomes. They are the body's way of flashing a caution sign, like the jolt of adrenaline we feel when we meet someone whose presence screams danger. This primal mechanism is rooted in survival, honed by evolution to protect us. However, it is important to navigate these signals with discernment. The phenomenon of unconscious bias refers to the way that past experiences and cultural or societal influences can affect our perception of people and events.

For instance, a hiring manager might select a candidate who graduated from the same college, not necessarily because of the school's reputation but because of an innate affinity for familiar backgrounds and cultural values. These subtle and seemingly innocuous unconscious biases can lead to unfair treatment and systemic inequalities. So, while our gut reactions can be protective, they may also echo silent prejudices and unexamined stereotypes. By acknowledging this duality, we create space to pause, peel back the layers of our immediate feelings, and weigh them against the scales of reason and empathy. By doing so, we honor the wisdom of our intuitions while elevating our decisions with the clear light of awareness. The following decision-making process can help fact-check your intuition by cross-referencing your actions with your values. However, if you intuit real danger, trust yourself and act fast.

A VALUES-BASED DECISION-MAKING PROCESS

Making decisions using your values requires deliberate effort at first, but with some practice, it will become frictionless and natural.

I recommend dedicating space for reflection, especially if you are making major life decisions. Don't make important decisions when hungover, after an argument, or in moments of heightened emotion, whether positive or negative. Relax, perhaps in nature, and deliberately activate your parasympathetic nervous system (rest and digest—remember the zebra!) before contemplating your next move.

While you can and should still trust your intuition, here is a methodology to give you peace of mind for those momentous decisions. You'll need paper and a pen, or you can download the interactive PDF from this web page: startwithvalues.com/decisions.

1. **Identify the Decision:** Clearly define the decision you need to make, keeping it as specific as possible.

2. **Confirm Your Core Values:** List your core values in order of priority.

3. **Explore Your Options:** List all possible actions that come to mind. Don't limit yourself; this is a brainstorming session.

4. **Options with Values:** Cross-reference each option with your core values. Score each option based on how many of your values it aligns with.

5. **Prioritize:** Is there an option that stands out as being most values-aligned? If not, you can add weight to the options that best align with your top value.

6. **Assess Impact:** Evaluate the broader consequences of each option. Consider how it will affect you and those around you, both in the short-term and in the long-term. Ask yourself: which option will bring me greater fulfillment?

7. **Take Action:** Choose the best-ranked option and act on it with confidence.

8. **Set a Review Date:** Put a reminder in your calendar to reassess your decision after an appropriate amount of time has passed.

9. **Reflect & Learn:** When the review date arrives, look back on the decision. Has it held up? Does it align with your values and produce the desired impact? What lessons can you draw for future decisions?

Values-based decision-making eliminates the paralysis often associated with major life choices because it reduces cognitive dissonance. When you know that the path you're choosing resonates with your values, the emotional toll associated with decision-making dissipates, replaced by a newfound sense of clarity and resolve. You can always course-correct if you've gone wrong. Values-aligned failures are incredible learning experiences.

Here is an advanced example of the decision-making process where we expand each option, writing down reasons why they're a good idea. Each reason is given a score out of ten and each value is weighted. Simply check the appropriate column when a reason is aligned with a value. Multiply your importance score by each checked value's score and then calculate a total for each reason. Subtotal the scores for each reason to get a final option score.

Decision: Should I purchase a new home?					
		Value 1	Value 2	Value 3	Score
Options	Importance	Fitness	Family	Adventure	
1. Purchase the new house	(score /10)	(worth 5 points)	(worth 4 points)	(worth 3 points)	
Why? Gives us more space	10	x	✓	x	40
Why? Excellent investment	8	x	✓	x	32
Why? Closer to the beach, can exercise more frequently	8	✓	✓	✓	96
Why? Daughter can cycle to school	8	✓	✓	x	40
				Subtotal	228
2. Stay where I am	(score /10)	(worth 5 points)	(worth 4 points)	(worth 3 points)	
Why? Less financial pressure	8	x	✓	✓	56
Why? We can go on holidays instead	8	x	✓	✓	56
Why? No stressful purchasing process	5	x	✓	X	40
				Subtotal	152

While the above scoring shows a clear winner in this decision, you can still ask the question: which option will bring me greater fulfillment? Or, consider asking: at the end of my life will I be proud that I made this decision?

Here's another example, where the reasons for each option have been matched so that we can see a clear comparison.

Decision: Which job offer should I accept?					
		Value 1	Value 2	Value 3	Score
Possible Options	Importance	Achievement	Wealth	Friendship	
1. Accept offer from company A	(score /10)	(worth 5 points)	(worth 4 points)	(worth 3 points)	
Why? Salary: Excellent salary	10	x	✓	x	40
Why? Culture: Competitive rather than collabora- tive culture	8	✓	x	x	40
Why? Opportunity: Limited career path opportunities	8	x	x	x	0
Why? Balance: Expectation to work long hours	6	x	x	x	0
Why? Proximity: Close to home and friends	6	x	x	✓	18
				Subtotal	98
2. Accept offer from company B	(score /10)	(worth 5 points)	(worth 4 points)	(worth 3 points)	
Why? Salary: Mid- range salary	10	x	x	x	0
Why? Culture: Collaborative and relaxed com- pany culture	8	x	x	✓	24

Why? Opportunity: Significant career path opportunities	8	✓	x	X	40
Why? Balance: Flexible and supportive	6	x	x	✓	18
Why? Proximity: Far from home and friends	6	x	x	x	0
				Subtotal	82

Based on the above, it's easy to decide. Take "Job A"—it meets the requirements for both remuneration and potential to be recognized for achievements.

By methodically aligning our decisions with our values, we not only bring coherence and fulfillment to our lives but also affirm our identity and what we stand for in the world. Decisions shaped by values are the architecture of a life well-lived.

For a downloadable decision-making worksheet, please visit: startwithvalues.com/decisions.

Action: What is a decision that you need to make? Can you utilize the above decision-making process to help you evaluate your options and reasons? This tool also works brilliantly in the corporate environment, so if your company has clear core values, you can test it out in the business context.

A VALUES-BASED
MINDFULNESS PRACTICE

Stop for a moment. Meditation is proven to support a clear and focused mind, allowing for more thoughtful and considered decisions. Stanford University School of Medicine conducted a study that shows meditation can lead to a 30% decrease in stress related symptoms that often lead to serious illness.

A simple practice such as the following one, repeated regularly, can reduce impulsive reactions and enhance your ability to weigh options with calmness and clarity.

1. Sit comfortably in a place where you feel at ease.

2. Set an intention: which of your top three core values will you meditate on?

3. Set an alarm, if you wish. 5 minutes is a good starting point.

4. Breathe in for four seconds and out for six seconds. Do this six times and then allow your breath to flow naturally.

5. Notice the sounds around you. Accept them. Let them go.

6. Notice your breathing. Tune into the natural rise and fall of your chest.

7. Notice your thoughts. Accept them. Let them go.

8. Give yourself a smile.

9. Consider your core value. Affirm your values-based identity by mentally stating, "I am a [value] person." For example: "I am a peaceful person."

10. Visualize yourself acting in alignment with this value. Be specific and conjure up a detailed situation in your mind's eye.

11. Now let go of the visualization. Give yourself a smile.

12. Notice your breathing. Tune into the rise and fall of your chest.

13. Notice your thoughts. Accept them. Let them go.

14. Give yourself a smile.

15. Notice the sounds around you.

16. Wiggle your fingers and toes, then gently open your eyes.

For a guided version of this practice, visit startwithvalues.com/meditation.

Action: How do you feel after dedicating a few mindful moments to one of your core values? Can you make this practice a micro-habit?

VALUES AND RITES OF PASSAGE

Rites of passage once punctuated the human experience, marking transformations with ceremonies and celebrations. From the solitude of a trial in the wilderness to the shared rituals of religious and communal celebrations, humans sought the wisdom of community and tradition to commemorate life's transitions.

At their essence, rites are a deliberate way to recognize the changing nature of a person's values. Today, the rites of marriage and funeral are observed for most people, but many others have been lost.

For example, transitioning from youth to adulthood was never solely about physical change; it was an ancestral echo, imparting duties, rights, and centuries-old wisdom. Ascending to leadership was a profound evolution from being a contributor to being a guardian and protector of the group.

Nowadays, our milestones are often reduced to a selfie or a LinkedIn update. These are quickly lost in the feed, and we dive into life's busyness without space to recognize—or fully comprehend—the change.

Rites provide:

- Anchors in the life experience.
- Recognition for who we have been and who we will become.
- Moments to express gratitude for the journey this far.
- A gravity that not only brings people together but signals the depth of our commitment to the new life on the other side of the transition.

Without rites, we risk feeling unmoored and lacking the guidance to adapt our values to new roles and responsibilities. In revaluing the power of rites, we do more than nod to bygone customs; we recognize the value shifts that life's stages bring. Intentionally crafted, these rites stand as profound acknowledgments of growth, guiding not just the individual's status but also his evolving values, ensuring his journey forward is as rich in meaning as it is in achievement.

Here are five examples of values-based rites of passage centered around moments or events when values often undergo transformation:

1. Entering Adulthood

Value Shift: From dependence to independence and responsibility.

Rite of Passage: A "Coming of Age" journey or retreat. This could be a guided trip where the individual is tasked with certain challenges (e.g., a wilderness hike, fasting, or solo reflection). Upon return, a communal gathering acknowledges his or her transition, and the individual shares his or her insights and commitments as an adult.

2. Marriage or Committing to a Life Partnership

Value Shift: From individuality to partnership, unity, and shared responsibility.

Rite of Passage: Beyond the wedding, a "Union Retreat" where the couple spends a weekend diving deep into their shared values, future plans, and mutual commitments. This may be facilitated by a counselor, spiritual leader, or simply guided by structured prompts for discussion.

3. Becoming a Parent

Value Shift: From individualism to nurturance and responsibility.

Rite of Passage: A "Welcoming Life" ceremony where close friends and family gather to share stories, hopes, and advice about parenthood with the expecting parents. Participants might gift books, share personal experiences, and offer blessings or intentions for the new family unit.

4. Assuming a Leadership Role at Work

Value Shift: From being an individual contributor to guiding and mentoring others.

Rite of Passage: A "Leadership Dedication" workshop. Colleagues and mentors come together to provide lessons on leadership, share stories, and set expectations. The new leader might create a vision board or a leadership manifesto as a tangible reminder of his or her new role.

5. Entering Retirement

Value Shift: From career-focused ambitions to legacy, reflection, and leisure.

Rite of Passage: A "Legacy Celebration" where the retiree gathers with family, friends, and colleagues to reminisce on career achievements, share stories, and articulate hopes for the next phase of life. This event can culminate in the creation of a legacy project or plan, detailing how the retiree wishes to contribute to his or her community or family in the post-career years.

Each of these rites of passage is designed to provide a structured and meaningful way to acknowledge and navigate value shifts, ensuring that we don't merely drift into new life stages but move forward with clarity, purpose, and community support.

> **Action:** What is a values-based rite of passage you can celebrate for yourself or someone you care about?

VALUES-BASED RITUALS

Rites of passage mark life's grand transitions, but rituals can help us to regularly honor and affirm our values. These rituals may be supported by the micro-habit process, especially when the ritual is new and you're deliberately working to embed it into your routine. However, rituals transcend habitual actions; they serve as deliberate pauses for introspection, appreciation, and awe.

Research promotes the significance of rituals. Psychological studies reveal that engaging in rituals can diminish anxiety, enhance performance, and strengthen communal bonds. One study highlighted that a pre-task ritual could alleviate anxiety and bolster self-belief. All this implies that rituals, even simple ones, are not trivial—they endow us with control and intention.

Consider Colonel William McRaven's advice to "make your bed." In his University of Texas commencement address and motivational book by that title, McRaven discusses how this simple ritual instills discipline, provides a sense of accomplishment, and introduces order to the day. It is also a gift to the future version of yourself, who is able to sleep in a beautifully-made bed that evening.

Rituals can embody our deepest values, doing more than just structuring our day but injecting meaningful action into our routine and reinforcing our sense of values alignment. Let's explore rituals for some commonly held values:

Value: Gratitude

Ritual: Each night before bed, write down three things you're thankful for from the day. This practice reinforces a perspective of appreciation and counters the human tendency to focus on negatives. It is also proven to improve sleep.

Value: Family

Ritual: Hold a weekly family dinner where all electronic devices are put away. This time is dedicated to sharing, listening, and connecting with each other.

Value: Community

Ritual: Volunteer at a local charity or community event once a month. This not only serves the community but reinforces the value of collective contribution.

Value: Peace

Ritual: Begin each day with 10 minutes of meditation or deep breathing exercises to center oneself and stay present.

Value: Nature Stewardship

Ritual: Take a weekly nature walk or hike. This can be a time of reflection, exercise, and reconnection with the environment. Bring a bag to collect any litter you encounter along the way.

Value: Creativity

Ritual: Dedicate an hour each week to a creative hobby, whether it's painting, writing, playing an instrument, or any other artistic pursuit.

Value: Respect

Ritual: Whenever you engage in a disagreement or debate, practice active listening without interrupting. After the other person has spoken, repeat back what you heard to ensure understanding.

Value: Generosity

Ritual: Set aside a small portion of your monthly income for charitable donations or random acts of kindness. This could be as simple as paying for someone's coffee in line behind you.

Value: Integrity

Ritual: At the end of each week, reflect on any instances where you might have compromised your integrity and consider ways to address and rectify them in the future.

Value: Adventure

Ritual: Once a month, try something new, whether it's a class, a hobby, or visiting a place you've never been before.

Want to craft your own ritual? Here is a methodology for you to follow.

HOW TO CREATE VALUES-BASED RITUALS

Crafting values-based rituals requires intention, reflection, and consistent practice. Shared rituals are positively potent, whether at home or work.

I worked with a bank where they wanted to create a culture of calm. They decided to implement one minute of calm before any meeting took place. At first, this was regarded as a wacky wellness fad—and was met with rolled eyes by many. However, after a few months, it became a ritual, something the bank employees really looked forward to. Beginning as simply an exercise in cultivating calm, it became a shared moment of contemplation and presence. Your micro-habits might naturally become rituals, but deliberately crafted practices are worth considering.

Here's a methodology to guide the creative process:

1. **Value Identification:** Begin by selecting one of your top core values; pinpoint a value that resonates deeply.

2. **Historical Reflection:** Look into traditional rituals from cultures around the world. How have they celebrated similar values? This isn't about appropriation but about understanding how universal values have been honored across time and space.

3. **Personal Relevance:** Ensure that the ritual is personally meaningful. It should resonate with your experiences, beliefs, and aspirations.

4. **Simplicity and Consistency:** Rituals don't have to be elaborate to be effective. Simple acts, done consistently, often hold the most power. For example, a daily moment of gratitude expressed at the same time can be a potent ritual.

5. **Integrate Sensory Experiences:** Involve the senses—sight, sound, smell, touch, and taste—to make the ritual more immersive. This could involve lighting a specific scented candle, playing a particular piece of music, or tasting something symbolic (dark chocolate is my favorite).

6. **Incorporate Symbolism:** Symbols provide a tangible or visual representation of the intangible. Choose symbols that best represent the value you're honoring—this could be an object, a gesture, or a phrase.

7. **Regular Reflection and Iteration:** Set aside time periodically to reflect on the ritual's effectiveness. Is it still serving its purpose?

Is it still aligned with the value it's meant to honor? Adjust as needed.

8. **Community Involvement (Optional):** If applicable, involve other members of your community or family. Shared rituals can strengthen bonds and reinforce shared values. For example, I have a ritual of touching a formation that looks like a face in a rock situated on one of my favorite running tracks. It started as a way to acknowledge nature's beauty. My wife and daughter have subsequently adopted the same ritual, expressing their own appreciation of the spot. A few days ago, I noticed a stranger touch the same rock as he walked past.

9. **Document the Ritual:** Write down the steps, symbols, and purpose of the ritual. This documentation can serve as a reminder and can be passed on to others who might find value in it.

10. **Commitment:** Rituals derive power from repetition and intention. Commit to practicing the ritual for a set period, understanding that its full impact might only become apparent over time.

By consciously creating rituals around our values, we provide ourselves with regular reminders of what is important to us, reinforcing our commitment to those values and integrating them more deeply into our daily lives.

> **Action:** Consider your top three values. What is a ritual that will enable you to honor one of your values on a regular basis?

CULTIVATING A VALUES-BASED ENVIRONMENT

The ambiance of a space tells the story of its values. The serene hush of a yoga studio, the energy of a nightclub's strobe lights and lasers, the solemn grandeur within a church's walls, or the stark sterility of a hospital corridor. Contrast the soft, embracing warmth of a newborn baby's nursery with a gym's mirrors and energizing artwork. Each space is an experience, whispering to us of the values it stands for, shaping our feelings and actions within it.

Here are the underlying values for each of the environments mentioned:

Yoga Studio

- Tranquility: To cultivate a peaceful mind.
- Harmony: Encouraging alignment between mind, body, and spirit.
- Simplicity: A minimalistic setting to reduce distractions and promote focus.

Dance Clubs

- Excitement: Pulsating lights and beats elevate adrenaline.
- Social Connection: Encouraging interactions and shared experiences.
- Escapism: A setting that allows patrons to momentarily forget daily routines.

Churches

- Reverence: Inspiring respect and veneration.
- Spirituality: Connection to the divine or a higher power.
- Tradition: Respecting and upholding long-standing rituals and practices.

Hospitals

- Sterility: Emphasizing cleanliness and reducing risk of infection.
- Efficiency: Organized in a manner that prioritizes swift and effective care.
- Safety: Ensuring patient and staff well-being.

Expectant Mother's Nursery

- Nurturing: Creating a safe and loving environment for the baby.
- Protection: Ensuring the baby is shielded from potential harm.
- Growth: Setting up a space conducive for development and learning.

Gym

- Motivation: Encouraging patrons to push their limits.
- Self-awareness: Mirrors to ensure correct posture and form.
- Achievement: Celebrating progress and milestones.

We can all integrate values into our environment. Drawing from user experience design, I'm excited to present a step-by-step guide for creating your values-based spaces.

Step 1: Create a Mood Board for Each Value

- **Gather Inspiration:** Collect images, color swatches, fabric samples, quotes, and any other items that resonate with each core value.
- **Assemble Mood Boards:** Create a physical or digital mood board for each value, compiling all the inspirational elements you've gathered.

Step 2: Explore Visual Themes

- **Identify Themes:** Look for recurring visual motifs in your mood boards, such as colors, patterns, and textures that capture the essence of your values.
- **Refine Palette:** Use these themes to refine a color palette and design an aesthetic that represents each value.

Step 3: Identify Symbols and Metaphors

- **Symbolic Elements:** Select symbols or metaphors that visually symbolize your values and integrate them into your mood boards.

Step 4: Select Artwork and Quotes

- **Curate Art and Text:** Choose artwork and quotes that align with the visual themes of your mood boards and add them to the composition.

Step 5: Choose Decorative Items

- **Decor Selection:** Based on your mood boards, select decorative items such as ornaments, posters, and textiles that will visually express your values in your environment.

Step 6: Plan Your Space

- **Spatial Planning:** Decide on the placement of these items in your space, considering factors such as visibility and the overall flow of the environment.

Step 7: Implementation

- **Acquire Items:** Begin purchasing or creating the decorative pieces you've chosen.
- **Decorate:** Start decorating your space, using the mood board as a visual guide to aesthetics and arrangement.

Step 8: Review and Iterate

- **Evaluate:** Step back and review your space once the items are in place, assessing whether the decorations effectively represent your values.
- **Iterative Process:** Be prepared to make adjustments, fine-tuning your space to better align with your values over time.

Step 9: Reinforce with Daily Interaction

- **Engage with Your Space:** Interact with the elements you've incorporated to ensure they remain meaningful and not just decorative.
- **Evolve:** Allow your space to change as you grow and as your understanding and expression of your values deepen.

This process encourages an active and evolving relationship with your values, ensuring that they are not only represented in your environment but are also lived and experienced daily.

> **Action:** How can you integrate your values into your home and office environment? The simplest way is to write out or print your top three values and stick them to your wall. Beyond that, it is a creative process—one that many will find deeply fulfilling.

NEUROAESTHETICS AND VALUES

Neuroaesthetics is a rapidly emerging interdisciplinary field that sits at the crossroads of art, neuroscience, and psychology. It seeks to decipher the neural mechanisms underpinning our aesthetic experiences, and how such experiences influence our emotions, cognition, and, by extension, our behaviors.

Our surroundings continuously interact with our senses, subtly shaping our mood, decisions, and actions. For instance, the principles of Zen, which emphasize simplicity, harmony, and nature, have influenced Japanese art and design for centuries. A Zen garden, with its raked sand and strategically placed rocks, is not just an aesthetic endeavor but a reflection of Zen values, promoting meditation, reflection, and inner calm. The environment, in its understated beauty, facilitates a deeper connection to these values.

In a similar vein, when our personal or communal spaces are thoughtfully curated to mirror our values, the aesthetic appeal does more than just satisfy our eyes. It engages our brain in a manner that reinforces these values, making them more accessible and salient in our daily life. For instance, someone who deeply values sustainability might decorate his home with upcycled materials and green plants. Every interaction within this space subtly reminds him of his commitment to the environment.

By consciously crafting environments that mirror our values, we create spaces that not only provide visual pleasure but also serve to reinforce our commitment to leading a values-aligned life. Consider communal plazas in Europe that promote community gathering, the intricate mandalas in Buddhist traditions symbolizing the universe and unity, or the minimalistic designs in Scandinavian homes emphasizing simplicity and functionality—these are all reflections of values translated into tangible aesthetics.

> **Action:** How do the environments you frequent reflect or support your values? Can you spend more time in places that align with what matters most to you?

MUSIC AND SOUND

I remember exploring my uncle's record collection as a child. The Pet Shop Boys, Bon Jovi and Queen filled me with emotions I had no name for. Lionel Ritchie sang soothing love songs and Madonna rebelled against conformity. To this day, I use music to support my values. For example, the sound of drum and bass or trance energizes my workouts, and spiritual chants help me to be present.

The field of music therapy taps into this force, with trained professionals using the therapeutic qualities of sound to aid in healing and improving life quality. Brainwave entrainment is the concept that rhythmic pulses of music can guide our brainwave patterns into synchronization, leading us to states of deep relaxation, heightened focus, or restful sleep, depending on the frequencies used. This alignment of our neural rhythms with a beat is a powerful testament to music's ability to alter our consciousness.

But the influence of music extends beyond brainwaves; it can play a critical role in emotion regulation. Upbeat tunes inject vigor and joy into our day, while slower, softer compositions invite calmness, providing a sanctuary for the mind in times of stress or contemplation. Music, especially instrumental music, offers a canvas for our feelings, letting us infuse our personal stories into the spaces between notes. In moments of pain or anxiety, music can also act as a lifeline, offering a mental escape route, or serving as an anchor, bringing us back to a place of stability.

But music is powerful, so use it with care. Playing that breakup playlist for too long after splitting from a partner can reinforce your sadness, leading to deeper despair.

CONNECTING SOUND TO VALUES

Just as you can structure a physical environment to reflect your values, so too can you shape Spotify to inject more aligned rhythms into your day. Here are some values, along with musical styles and genres, that can support alignment. To listen to my playlists, visit bradleyhook. com/music.

1. **Creativity:** If you value creativity, you might find inspiration in genres like jazz, where improvisation is central, rap for rhymes, or classical compositions. Listening to music from different cultures can also expand your creative horizons, exposing you to new rhythms, instruments, languages and melodic structures.

2. **Focus:** Those who value focus and concentration might lean towards white noise, brown noise, or specific frequencies designed to promote concentration. Classical music, particularly pieces with a consistent tempo and no vocals like Bach's compositions, can enhance cognitive processing.

3. **Spirituality:** If spirituality is a core value, chants, hymns, or meditative music might resonate deeply.

4. **Community:** Try folk music, with its rich tradition of storytelling and communal singing.

5. **Fitness:** There's a reason why gyms play high-energy electronic dance music—it gets us moving. However, some people prefer old-school rock or metal to fuel their workouts.

In conclusion, the sounds we surround ourselves with can profoundly influence our emotional and cognitive states. By curating a sound environment that resonates with our values, we not only enhance our daily experiences but also create a sonic space that keeps us aligned.

> **Action:** Craft a playlist to support each of your top three values. Switch it on when you want to move to the rhythm of what matters most.

THE IMPORTANCE OF PERSONAL WELL-BEING

Through my work at the Resilience institute, I've presented health and well-being workshops and seminars to audiences around the world for over a decade. Without a foundation of physical, mental, and emotional health, being resilient and making decisions that reflect your values is challenging. Research shows that a holistic approach to well-being—encompassing nutrition, movement, and sleep—enhances overall health and supports the mental clarity and energy needed for values-based living.

Diets, New Year's resolutions, and health goals usually fail, whereas tiny habitual changes lead to significant improvements in quality of life over time. I aim to assist people in overcoming their natural resistance to change by developing values-based micro-habits that extend their health span—the length of time they live without chronic illness—and provide lifelong vitality.

Here is my simple guide to wellness:

Sleep: Aim for 7-8 hours per night. Turn off bright lights in the evening and follow the 3-2-1 process:

- 3 hours before bed, stop eating.
- 2 hours before bed, stop drinking.
- 1 hour before bed, stop scrolling.

Move

- Aim to move every single day.
- Mix up your movement by incorporating flexibility, strength, cardio, balance, and high intensity. If you can't find time for 30 minutes of movement per day, either fitness is not a value, you're ridiculously busy, or you're struggling to get started.
- Start with a 1-minute micro-habit to bypass your resistance and gradually increase as the habit becomes enjoyable and robust.

Breathe: Tune into your breathing patterns and breathe intentionally at least once daily. Slow your breath, create some space, and enjoy the benefits of a mindful moment—sometimes called a "glimmer"—to disrupt the runaway mind and signal safety to the nervous system.

Eat: Avoid highly processed foods. That's pretty much everything in the middle aisles of a supermarket. If possible, explore locally-produced food options and do your best to reduce the consumption of produce treated with pesticides and toxic chemicals. Try growing some food yourself—it can be very fulfilling, even if it is just a few herbs.

A MORNING ROUTINE BY DESIGN (NOT BY DEFAULT)

A quick and easy way to boost your well-being is through a deliberately constructed morning routine. My suggested routine integrates various practices supported by research across psychology, neuroscience, and preventative medicine:

1. **Hydrate with water and salt:** Start your day by drinking a glass of water mixed with a pinch of Celtic sea salt or Himalayan rock salt. Popularized by Professor Andrew Huberman, this practice replenishes essential minerals and kickstarts your metabolism.

2. **Grounding:** Spend a few minutes connecting with the earth, either by standing barefoot on the ground or using a grounding mat. Once considered "new age," this research-supported practice can reduce inflammation and improve mood, giving you a solid start to the day.

3. **Breathing exercises:** Practice deep breathing or Tactical Calm (inhale for 4 seconds, exhale for 6 seconds) for a few minutes to oxygenate your body and calm your mind.

4. **Morning sunlight exposure:** Spend a few minutes outside in the morning sunlight to regulate your circadian rhythm and boost vitamin D levels.

5. **Stretching:** Incorporate a few minutes of stretching to wake up your muscles and increase flexibility.

Integrating these steps into your morning routine will enhance your well-being and provide a foundation for a values-based day.

> **Action:** What will improve your well-being: sleep, movement, diet, or breathwork? Design an intentional morning routine that works for you.

VISUALIZATION AND VALUES

If the idea of visualization has you thinking of *The Secret* or mystical manifestation techniques, think again. The most decorated Olympian of all time, swimmer Michael Phelps, used visualization to enhance his swimming performance, eventually winning 28 Olympic medals. He would vividly imagine every detail of the forthcoming race, from his starting dive to each stroke and turn, ensuring he was mentally prepared for any scenario, including unexpected challenges. This practice not only helped him stay calm and focused during competitions, but also gave him the hope and optimism that he could overcome any obstacle, ultimately contributing to his success.

When I run seminars for large audiences, the nerves inevitably kick in a few minutes before I am due to step on stage. I discovered that deliberate visualization shifts my emotional state from anxiety to excitement and readiness. A technique I find helpful is to imagine the audience applauding after participating in what will be an inspiring and entertaining experience. The key is to imagine myself in the room after the presentation, smiling, relaxed, and playful, feeling gratitude for the opportunity to serve others and share my ideas. After that brief 10-second visualization, I noticeably relax. The vision of success actually prepares me for the unfolding reality.

Visualization is not just a self-help technique. It's a scientifically proven tool for goal achievement and values-based living. When we deliberately imagine our desired outcomes in elaborate detail, we enhance our motivation and increase our resilience. Psychology and neuroscience research have shown that mental rehearsal activates the same neural pathways as physical practice, leading to improved skills and a growth mindset.

Insights from David Robson's excellent book *The Expectation Effect* further highlight how our beliefs and expectations can shape our reality. For example, a cyclist achieved his personal best after believing he had taken a performance-enhancing drug, which was just a saline solution. This phenomenon is closely related to the placebo effect, where positive expectations lead to beneficial outcomes, and the nocebo effect, where negative expectations can cause harm. When we visualize positive outcomes, we create a mental blueprint that our brain strives to follow.

It is worth highlighting the role of the Reticular Activating System (RAS). The RAS is a network of neurons in the brainstem that filters information and prioritizes what we focus on. Visualization strengthens the RAS, making it more attuned to recognizing opportunities and resources that align with our goals and values. By consistently practicing visualization, we can train our RAS to filter out distractions—including unhelpful thought patterns—and focus on what truly matters: values-aligned action that leads us toward a life of fulfillment.

We used basic visualization in our meditation practice earlier. Here are some additional visualization practices and how to use them effectively:

1. **Vision Boarding:** Create a collage of images and words representing your goals and values. Place it somewhere you'll see it daily to remind you of your aspirations.

2. **Guided Imagery:** Listen to guided imagery recordings that take you through achieving your goals. These can help you relax and focus your mind on positive outcomes.

3. **Mental Rehearsal:** Spend a few minutes each day visualizing yourself successfully achieving your goals. Use all your senses to create a vivid, detailed picture in your mind.

To visualize effectively, follow these steps:

- **Set Clear Intentions:** Define what you want to achieve and why it's important. For example, "I value serving others, so I will complete my certificate in nutrition coaching."
- **Use All Senses:** Imagine the sights, sounds, smells, tastes, and feelings associated with your desired outcome. Based on the example above, you might visualize yourself celebrating with a coaching client who has transformed his health and well-being.
- **Practice Regularly:** Dedicate a few minutes each day to your visualization practice to maintain focus and momentum. An excellent time for this is during your morning routine. Remember, attach new habits to those that are already reliable.

> **Action:** Whether you value fitness, service, social connection, or status, spend a few moments conjuring up a mental movie of a specific values-based achievement. For example, if you value friendship, visualize how great it will feel after reaching out to one friend per week for the next month. This will help you prioritize the activity, even if you feel some resistance.

THE RISK OF EXTREME VALUES-ALIGNMENT

There are many examples of extreme values-alignment. While it can lead to mastery and service, extreme alignment can also lead to tragedy. Imagine a person so devoted to values of strength, loyalty, and unity that he founded one of the largest empires in history. The result was extensive cultural exchange and a flourishing of important trade routes. The side effects of this achievement included incalculable devastation, demise, and suffering. This person was Genghis Khan. Cities that would not yield to his vision of a vast interconnected empire were razed to the ground, and their inhabitants slaughtered. His genetic legacy continues, with a 2003 study finding that 8% of Asian men (0.5% of the world population) carry his Y chromosome.

While this is an extreme example, it clearly illustrates the fact that seemingly noble values can cause immense suffering due to the morals and beliefs driving decision-making.

Let's explore five common examples of values that can be taken to the extreme, with potentially detrimental effects:

- **Compassion Overdose:** At its core, compassion involves understanding and alleviating the suffering of others. Yet, when taken to an extreme, it can lead to emotional exhaustion or "compassion fatigue." Individuals might find themselves perpetually giving of themselves, transgressing or destroying their personal boundaries, exhausting their reserves, and ultimately neglecting their well-being and burning out in the service of others.
- **Innovation at All Costs:** While innovation drives progress and encourages out-of-the-box thinking, an unbridled focus on constant novelty can lead to instability. Organizations or individuals overly focused on innovation might find themselves perpetually

chasing the next big thing, overlooking the foundational elements that ensure stability.

- **Perfection Pursuit**: The aim for perfection is like chasing the horizon—the closer you seem to get, the further away it moves. Valuing perfection is about striving for excellence and quality, but when it morphs into an obsession, it can paralyze you. You might end up in a loop of endless tweaking and tuning, never satisfied, never done. Or you might criticize others harshly for failing to meet your unrealistic expectations. It's the perfect trap—because when nothing is ever good enough, nothing ever gets finished.

- **Freedom Extremes**: Freedom is the open road, the wind in your hair, the choice to take any turn you want. It's essential for creativity, personal growth, and happiness. But push freedom to the limit, and you'll find chaos. This can lead to a lack of responsibility, aimlessness, or even harm to oneself and others. Like an untethered kite without something to anchor it, unbridled freedom can just fly away or crash.

- **Competitive Edge**: Competition can light a fire under you, keep you moving, and keep you sharp. But when winning becomes everything, you might start to cut corners, step over others, or lose sight of why you're playing the game to begin with. In the relentless pursuit of victory, relationships can suffer, ethics can take a back seat, and ironically, you can end up losing what you sought to gain—respect, integrity, and true success.

Each of these examples reveals a profound truth: values are like spices in a dish—the right amount can create something incredible, but too much and it's all you can taste, overpowering everything else.

Ancient wisdom offers insights into the importance of balance. The Chinese philosophy of Yin and Yang emphasizes the interconnected and interdependent nature of dualities. Just as there is a bit of Yin within Yang and vice versa, our values, too, should be in harmonious balance. Intensity and recovery, action and reflection, giving and receiving—these are all dualities that require equilibrium for sustained well-being. Just as a recipe needs a blend of ingredients to create a perfect dish, our values, too, function best when they're harmonized with other dimensions of our character. For instance, compassion can be complemented by boundaries and self-care, ensuring that we don't overextend ourselves.

Action: Which of your values could cause you or others distress if taken to the extreme? What are some actions you can take to find and maintain balance?

5

COMMUNICATE YOUR VALUES

IN THE FALL of 1985, two world leaders met in Geneva: Ronald Reagan, President of the United States, and Mikhail Gorbachev, General Secretary of the Soviet Union. These two countries, both armed with nukes, had been entrenched in ideological warfare—the Cold War—for decades. As a child growing up, I truly believed a nuclear winter was inevitable. I desperately hope that, no matter when you are reading this book, this has never become a reality.

In a private meeting between the two leaders, the conversation shifted from geopolitics to values and beliefs. Reagan recounted tales of freedom, individual rights, and the dreams of ordinary Americans. In turn, Gorbachev spoke of peace, the future of Soviet children, and his aspirations for his country's place in the world. For a brief moment, the weight of nuclear codes and political influence gave way to shared humanity.

Their connection laid the foundation for successive summits and, eventually, pivotal arms reduction treaties. This wasn't just high-stakes diplomacy; this was values-based communication in action.

In the next section, we'll explore ways to clearly articulate your core values and how to discover someone else's.

ARTICULATE YOUR VALUES

Giving voice to your values requires preparation and courage. Values-based conversation is easy with people who share the same values—that's why we gravitate toward specific communities, political parties, and spiritual systems. Beyond the safety of our in-group, our values can and will be met with resistance out in an opinionated world.

You need to decide what level of tolerance you have for criticism and how fiercely you are willing to defend your position. Are you valiant? Are you the hero of your journey, or will you play a supporting role—an important thing to do—in someone else's journey? Will you regret not speaking up?

Voicing your values doesn't necessarily require broadcasting them on social media, wearing them on a badge, or announcing them to someone you have just met. Some people do, and it can be overbearing, especially if you don't share the same values.

There are jokes about vegans wanting to let you know they are vegan within the first few minutes of a meeting. If you're not vegan, you might feel judged, do some judging, or simply not care. Imagine if you could understand *why* this person chose veganism as a lifestyle. This could form the basis of an enriching conversation—perhaps even revealing that you share some underlying core values. After all, veganism could be driven by sustainability, care (for animals), kindness, health reasons, or belonging (to a group). By discovering the underlying value, you open a pathway to deeper connection and understanding. Later, we'll explore how to uncover someone else's values, but first, let's explore how to clearly articulate your own.

This ability will build trust, show you are clear about what you want, and remove ambiguity. But simply stating your value might be confusing. For example, "integrity" can mean different things to different people. The more precisely you can define what your value means to you, the easier it will be to explain it to someone else. Here is a process to help you:

1. **Define the Value:** Start by defining what the value means to you. Take "integrity," for instance—perhaps in your experience it means honesty, ethical behavior, or transparency.

2. **Identify Behaviors:** Once you've defined the value, list behaviors or actions that reflect this value. For integrity, this might mean returning extra change given to you by mistake or admitting when you're wrong.

3. **Craft a Statement:** Create a statement that encapsulates these behaviors. Instead of just saying "I value integrity," you could say, "I believe in doing the right thing, even when no one is watching." This adds layers of meaning and specificity to the value, making it actionable.

4. **Test the Statement:** Imagine different scenarios where this statement could guide your behavior. For example, would this integrity statement prompt you to speak out against a popular but ethically dubious trend? Would it inspire you to confess that you made a mistake at work, even if you might face repercussions?

Let's explore some examples of values being converted into easily communicable statements.

1. **Integrity:** In a job interview: "For me, integrity is a cornerstone of how I approach my work. I'm committed to delivering what I promise, and I stand by my word."

2. **Empathy:** With a friend: "I try to approach relationships with empathy, so if I ever say or do something that upsets you, please know that wasn't my intention and I'd like to understand how I can make it right."

3. **Curiosity:** In a team meeting: "I'm always eager to learn more about how things work or how they could be improved. If anyone has suggestions or new perspectives, I'm all ears!"

4. **Responsibility:** In a family setting: "I value being responsible, so I would like to take on the task of managing our family's finances."

5. **Adventure:** On a first date: "One of my core values is adventure; I love stepping out of my comfort zone and trying new experiences. How about you?"

6. **Sustainability:** At a community meeting: "I value sustainability and believe we should be good stewards of our environment. What steps can our community take to be more eco-friendly?"

7. **Financial Security:** With a financial planner: "Financial security is really important to me. I'm looking for investment strategies that provide a stable return."

8. **Work-Life Balance:** During a performance review: "Work-life balance is essential for me to perform at my best. Could we discuss flexible working options?"

9. **Creativity:** To a colleague: "I value creativity and love solving problems in unconventional ways. That's why I enjoy activities that challenge me to think outside the box."

Remember, use everyday language, share personal stories or examples, and avoid jargon that makes the values too abstract. The more you practice, the better you'll get, so start in low-risk environments with friends, family, and colleagues you trust. By actively living, articulating, and sharing your values, you not only construct a life that feels authentically "you," but you also encourage those around you to live with authenticity.

> **Action:** Communicate one of your values to someone using a clear and simple statement. Start with a trusted friend or family member, then try it out in a higher-stakes situation.

HOW TO DISCOVER SOMEONE ELSE'S VALUES

Discovering what drives other people can dramatically improve your relationships and influence. A great starting point is asking simple questions like:

- "What does success look like to you?"
- "How does it make you feel?"
- "Why is that important to you?"

Going deeper, you can ask questions like:

- "Can you describe a moment when you felt truly fulfilled or satisfied? What were you doing?"
- "Who do you admire most, and what qualities about them do you see as significant?"
- "When have you felt the proudest of yourself or your actions?"
- "What activities make you lose track of time, and why do you think they have that effect on you?"
- "What are non-negotiables in your life, things you wouldn't give up or compromise on?"
- "If you could change one thing about the world, what would it be, and what does this desire say about you?"
- "Can you tell me about a difficult decision you've had to make and how you approached it?"
- "What do you hope people say about you when you're not in the room, and why?"
- "Looking back at your life, what have been the most consistent themes or passions, and how do they shape your goals?"
- "What does a well-lived life look like to you, and what steps are you taking to achieve that?"

Another method is the "Five Whys" technique, which we've referenced a few times already in this book. Originally part of lean manufacturing, this method has been adapted to problem-solving, root cause analysis, and understanding deeper motivations in various settings, including psychology and personal development. The premise is simple: ask "Why?" five times in succession to drill down into the core reason or cause of a particular problem or situation.

Here's a simplified example in a personal context:

Question 1: Why do you want to change jobs?

"Because I'm not happy at my current job."

Question 2: Why are you not happy at your current job?

"Because I don't feel like I'm using my skills to the fullest."

Question 3: Why don't you feel like you're using your skills?

"Because my job is repetitive and doesn't challenge me."

Question 4: Why does a lack of challenge bother you?

"Because I feel like I'm not growing or learning new things."

Question 5: Why is growth important to you?

"Because I value self-improvement and making an impact."

By the end of the fifth "why," we've gone from a surface-level problem ("I'm not happy at my current job'") to uncovering a core value or motivation that is causing dissatisfaction ("I value self-improvement and making an impact").

The number of times you ask "why" doesn't have to be exactly five; the key is to continue asking until you reach the root cause or discover a core value or belief. This technique can be an insightful way to better understand someone's values or motivations, whether in a personal or professional setting.

There are, of course, other ways to discover someone's values. Here are some pointers:

- **Observation:** Before diving into direct questioning, spend time respectfully observing the person in various situations. How they behave in diverse contexts can offer clues to their values. For example, someone who consistently chooses to spend free time reading or engaging in intellectual conversations likely values 'Intellectual Growth' or 'Curiosity.'

- **Active Listening:** Pay attention not just to what the other person is saying, but also to the underlying messages or themes. Are they always talking about adventures, experiences, or taking risks? These could be signs pointing to values like 'Adventure,' 'Experience,' or 'Risk-Taking.'

- **Ask Open-Ended Questions:** Instead of yes-or-no questions, ask open-ended ones that encourage reflection and discussion. Questions like, "What matters most to you?" or "What would your ideal day look like?" can elicit responses that reveal core values.

- **Use Hypothetical Scenarios:** Pose hypothetical situations and ask what they would do. For example, "If you won the lottery today, what would you do with the money?" Or, "If you lost all of your money today, what would you do?" The answers can help you understand their priorities and, by extension, their values.

- **Note Their Reactions in High-Stakes Situations:** Pay attention to how they respond in stressful or high-stakes circumstances. Whether it's a difficult project at work or a family crisis, these situations often reveal true colors and underlying values.

- **Be Direct But Tactful:** If you've built enough rapport, you could straightforwardly ask what they value most in life. However, this requires a certain level of trust and openness, so use your judgment on when it's appropriate to be this direct. (Refer friends to this book if they are interested. I'd really appreciate that.)

- **Analyze Choices and Decisions:** The choices one makes often directly reflect underlying values. Whether it's a career move, investment, or even the kind of friendships they cultivate, these decisions are laden with clues about what they value most.

- **Leverage Shared Experiences:** When you engage in activities together, observe what excites them, what they ignore, and what they criticize. Shared experiences can be incredibly revealing.

The process of discovering someone else's values isn't a one-time event but an ongoing process. Keep in mind that not everyone thinks about values in the same way that you do; many people have only a vague or subconscious sense of their core values. By considering their values more deliberately and consciously, you might reach a point where you are more aware of another person's values than they are themselves.

As you gather this insight, not only will your understanding of the other person deepen, but you'll also be better positioned to build a relationship rooted in mutual respect and shared values.

Action: Try to discover the core values of someone you care about.

COURAGEOUS VALUES-BASED CONVERSATIONS

Conflicts can arise when there's a mismatch or misunderstanding of core values. Navigating these differences requires a special kind of conversation—one that dives deep into the realm of values and beliefs to find common ground. Here is a practical approach to having courageous values-based conversations.

1. Preparation for the Discussion

- **Self-Reflection:** Before initiating a conversation, reflect on your own values. Understand what's driving your feelings and reactions. Ask yourself: "What core belief or value is being triggered or challenged?"

- **Open-Mindedness:** Approach the conversation with an open heart and mind. Be ready to listen, learn, and potentially adjust your perspective.

2. Articulating Your Values During Conflict

- **Be Specific:** Instead of saying, "I don't agree with that," try articulating the underlying value. For example, "I value transparency, and I feel this decision wasn't communicated openly."

- **Avoid Blame:** Frame your statements using "I" rather than "you." This way, you can express your feelings and values without pointing fingers or making the other person defensive.

- **Ask Open-Ended Questions:** Encourage dialogue by asking questions that don't have a "yes" or "no" answer. For example, "How do you see this decision aligning with our shared goal of innovation?"

3. Clarifying Someone Else's Values

- **Active Listening:** Give the other person your full attention. Listen not just to the words, but the emotions and values behind them.

- **Ask Clarifying Questions:** If you're unsure about the values driving someone's stance, ask them directly. For instance, "Can you help me understand the values that are guiding your perspective on this?"

- **Paraphrase:** Repeat back what you've heard in your own words. This ensures you've correctly understood and gives them a chance to clarify. For example, "To make sure that I understood you correctly, you're saying that innovation sometimes requires making changes without involving the whole team?"

4. Finding Common Ground

- **Highlight Shared Values:** Even in disagreement, there are often underlying shared values. Pointing these out can be a bridge to finding a solution. For instance, "We both value the success of this project, so let's find a way to address our concerns and move forward."

- **Agree to Disagree:** Sometimes, you might not reach an agreement, and that's okay. What's essential is understanding and respecting each other's values.

5. Closing the Discussion

- **Express Gratitude:** Thank the other person for sharing their perspective and values. It takes courage to engage in challenging conversations.

- **Action Steps:** If the discussion was about a specific conflict or decision, outline the next steps or areas of compromise based on the shared values and understandings unearthed during the conversation.

Incorporating values into courageous conversations leads to richer, more impactful connection. It's not just about resolving conflicts but deepening understanding and strengthening relationships. When we take the time to understand and honor the values of others, we lay the groundwork for social fitness and more collaborative, respectful, effective interactions with the people in our lives.

> **Action:** Do you need to have a courageous conversation? Can you leverage the process listed above?

QUICK RECAP

You've gained clarity on your values and understand the fight-or-flight responses triggered by perceived threats. You've learned to temper the stress response, keeping it from clouding your judgment. With a values-based identity, you now possess the capacity to swiftly utilize your values as lenses, rapidly turning challenges and decisions into manageable and meaningful actions. You also know that, from time to time, you may encounter real adversity and will need to address survival values before you broaden your perspective to values that bring deep engagement or help you thrive.

You courageously express and embody your values in your inter-actions with others. You're on a quest, your own hero's journey, and are excited about the authenticity this infuses into your life. Practice is key, but it's worth it. Living your values is valiant.

6

COLLECTIVE VALUES

WHEN I REFLECT on the friends I've had throughout my life, I read a story of shared and evolving values. The people I befriended had vastly different backgrounds, occupations, and beliefs, but we were united—at least for a time—by values. When I valued adventure, friendships made with fellow travelers just clicked, regardless of our backgrounds. "Normal people" who valued stability and consistency seemed quite alien. Today, while I still enjoy adventure, I sincerely appreciate stability and consistency within my family life.

Perhaps you've found yourself bonding effortlessly with someone who doesn't share your hobbies, musical tastes, or sports preferences. At a glance, it might seem puzzling, but when we dig deeper, the connection often lies in a shared value or two. When you share core values *and* favorite activities or interests with someone, you likely have a best friend.

FIND YOUR VALUES OVERLAP

The following is an insightful process to help you discover and articulate shared values, but please be tactful. Not everyone is interested in introspection, and some may dismiss the concept of values entirely. However, if you're in a romantic relationship, I highly recommend finding your values overlap before committing to marriage. Let's get started:

1. **Self-Reflection:** Before diving into a discussion about shared values, it's essential for each individual to have clarity about his or her own values. Take time separately to jot down each of your top three values. You may need to expand your lists to five values to find more overlaps.

2. **Open Discussion:** Once both parties have a clear sense of their individual values, come together for an open and honest conversation. Share your values and listen actively to your partner's values. The aim is not to judge or persuade, but to understand.

3. **Identify the Overlap:** As you converse, you'll likely discover areas where your values align, which I term as the "values overlap." These shared values become the pillars of your relationship, the common ground upon which mutual respect and understanding are built.

4. **Address the Differences:** It's natural to have values that don't align perfectly. Rather than viewing these differences as obstacles, consider them areas for growth and understanding. Discuss how you can respect and appreciate these differences.

5. **Craft a Relationship Values Statement:** Using your shared values as a foundation, work together to create a relationship values statement. You might not need to do this with your drinking buddies, but it is definitely worthwhile with your spouse. Your values statement should be a concise and affirmative declaration of the principles that will guide your relationship. It will serve as a touchstone you can return to, especially during challenging times, to remind you both of what you hold dear.

For example, a couple might come up with a statement like: "In our relationship, we value mutual respect, continual growth, and shared adventures. We commit to supporting one another in our individual pursuits."

This values statement becomes a powerful tool, reminding both individuals of the shared commitments and aspirations that brought them together and continue to strengthen their bond.

Examples of relationship statements that include acknowledgement of differing values are listed below.

1. **As siblings, we value kindness, respect, stability, and spontaneity.** We live these by supporting each other unconditionally while embracing our differences, enriching our bond and growth.

2. **As business partners, we value innovation, integrity, and collaboration.** We live these by fostering creative solutions, maintaining ethical practices, and working synergistically towards our common goals, ensuring our venture thrives on trust and inventive spirit.

3. **As a couple, we value fun, safety, and freedom.** We live these values by celebrating joy, honoring our unique perspectives, and respecting our individual needs, which strengthens our shared experiences.

FAMILY VALUES

Imagine your family as a ship navigating through the vast ocean of life. For both parents and children, shared values serve as the stars by which you chart your course—a celestial guide that promises stability and coherence. Without them, your ship may drift aimlessly or, worse, run aground when adversity strikes. It's not just about keeping afloat; it's about choosing your direction and pursuing it with intention. Everyone on board has a role to play, and clear values ensure that each person understands their duties. Values-aligned action strengthens the bonds of teamwork, trust, and shared purpose.

Your family's set of values is a living manuscript, continuously written by the choices you make and the lessons you teach. What will the chapters of your family story recount? Which profound insights will your descendants glean from the pages of your lived experiences?

In the end, the truest wealth you can leave behind is the legacy of strong values—stars that will light the way for generations to come.

Crafting Family Values

Here is how to co-create a set of family values.

Discovery

1. **Open Dialogue:** Initiate regular family discussions where each member can voice his or her opinions, feelings, and beliefs. This open platform can unearth shared values and shed light on differences.

2. **Reflect on Traditions:** Look back at family traditions, celebrations, and rituals. These are often rooted in values passed down through generations.

3. **Evaluate Challenges:** Consider situations when family members disagreed or faced dilemmas. Understanding the motivations behind choices can reveal underlying values.

Defining and Articulating Values

1. **Consolidate Common Themes:** From your discoveries, list recurring themes. This could include values like honesty, hard work, respect, or community service.

2. **Prioritize:** It's essential not to overwhelm, especially children, with an exhaustive list. Instead, prioritize and focus on the core values that resonate most with the family. Remember the rule of three.

3. **Craft a Family Values Statement:** This is a concise, clear declaration of what your family stands for. It acts as a reference point and a reminder for all members.

Communicating to Children and Defining Values-Based Behaviors

1. **Lead by Example:** Children learn more from what they see than what they hear. Be a role model by embodying the values you preach.

2. **Narrative Learning:** Share stories, both personal and fictional, that align with your family values. Narratives can make abstract values more tangible and relatable.

3. **Positive Reinforcement:** Praise and reward behaviors that align with your family values. This can motivate children to act according to these values.

4. **Open Discussions:** Encourage children to share their experiences related to family values. This not only reinforces the values but also develops their analytical and communicative skills.

While individual relationships, such as those between friends or romantic partners, can acknowledge and celebrate differences in values, the dynamics within a family setting often benefit from a more unified approach.

Examples of Family Values Statements

For clarity and cohesion, it's beneficial to distill a family values statement down to just three core values. This creates a focused blueprint for family decisions, behaviors, and traditions. Here are some examples:

1. **Religious family: "Our family values faith, tradition, and service.** We live these values by aligning our lives with our religious beliefs, honoring our ancestral traditions, and actively serving our community with love and compassion."

2. **Creative family: "Our family values expression, curiosity, and innovation.** We live these values by embracing artistic freedom, pursuing new experiences with an eagerness to learn, and fostering originality and fresh perspectives in our everyday lives."

3. **Progressive family: "Our family values equality, sustainability, and open-mindedness.** We live these values by advocating for everyone's rights, making eco-friendly choices, and welcoming diverse viewpoints and changes with a willingness to grow and learn."

It's important to remember that these are just examples, and the actual process of defining family values is deeply personal. It requires introspection, open dialogue, and mutual understanding among all family members. However, with dedication and communication, it's a journey that can fortify the familial bond like no other.

WORKPLACE VALUES

An organization where I worked onboarded a star performer—let's call her Anna. She excelled at everything, demonstrating commitment, passion and customer-centricity. A change in management changed everything. The company shifted from a values-based culture to a traditional productivity-focused culture. Anna's wings were clipped by micro-management, meetings and excessive detail. She lost her confidence. One day she told me, "I used to feel like this was my purpose, but now it's just a job." It wasn't just her. The company lost its way. Eventually, they shifted back to a values-based culture, integrating the tools and processes gained by a productivity focus— and they rebounded remarkably.

Studies by institutions like EY Beacon Institute, Harvard Business Review, and Gallup highlight that purpose-driven companies not only achieve higher revenue growth but also boast enhanced employee engagement, customer loyalty, and long-term strategic thinking. During economic downturns, these organizations demonstrate greater resilience, with some outperforming the general stock market by a significant margin. An emphasis on values and societal impact also garners higher trust among stakeholders—especially younger employees—further cementing the case for values-based, purpose-oriented business approaches.

So, if values are undeniably impactful, why have they been reduced to buzzwords in so many corporate settings? For many employees, the mere mention of "core values" can trigger an eye roll. It's the classic case of talk-the-talk minus walk-the-walk, leaving a trail of cynicism. When lofty words displayed on a company's website or walls do not align with actual leadership behaviors, the disconnect can foster an environment of distrust, sabotaging the power of values to drive change and secure a unified vision. For values to be meaningful, they cannot just be slogans—they need to be lived every day. When companies treat values as mere branding exercises without integrating them into the fabric of their operations and culture, they inadvertently contribute to the skepticism surrounding the term.

Reinvigorating Company Values

Reinvigorating existing company values necessitates more than a mere terminological overhaul; it requires a deep and committed process of discovery and alignment, just as we did for ourselves in previous sections of this book.

The first step in this revitalization process is deep introspection, looking critically at the current company values. Do they still resonate with the mission and vision of the organization, especially given its contemporary challenges and aspirations? It's a roundtable moment—bring everyone in, from the factory to the corner office. If the values aren't strumming the heartstrings of your mission and vision anymore, then it's time for a tune-up.

The active involvement of leadership is pivotal in this journey. Values without leader-champions are like a rudderless ship. When leaders embody the values, they don't just talk the talk; they set the stage for an entire culture to walk along with them. That's when values stop being posters and start being cornerstones.

But the real magic is in the everyday. Values should be the lens through which every business decision is made, the measuring stick for every project, the checklist for every new hire. Imagine interviewing not just for smarts but for heart, for that spark of shared values. What keeps these values alive and prevents them from becoming mere wall decorations is continuous communication and celebration. The power of storytelling cannot be understated here. Narrating real-world instances where values played a pivotal role in achieving milestones can transform these abstract concepts into tangible, relatable tales. This not only reinforces their importance but also makes them more accessible to the employees.

Training also plays a role in this reinvigoration process. By offering workshops that unpack the behaviors supporting each value, employees will be equipped with the necessary tools to act in alignment with them. Establishing feedback mechanisms where employees can share their experiences and interpretations of these values ensures that these principles are continually refined and remain relevant. A Slack or Teams channel will do just fine. Ask senior leaders to post regularly to keep the thread alive.

Lastly, recognition goes a long way in reinforcing the significance of values. By celebrating and rewarding those who demonstrate values-aligned decision-making and behavior, organizations not only motivate others to emulate these behaviors but also underline the pivotal role values play in the company's success narrative. Through a combination of introspection, leadership involvement, integration, communication, training, feedback, and recognition, companies can ensure their values are not just words, but the very lifeblood of their culture.

Co-Creating Company Values

Traditional models of determining company values—often driven by HR, marketing, or the leadership team—can miss the mark spectacularly. Co-created values are more inclusive and participatory; with tools like the Values App (startwithvalues.com/values-app), this approach is not only feasible but also highly effective.

The elegance of the Values App is its ability to clarify the core values of each individual in an organization. Employees take an assessment that reveals their personal values, then companies receive a Group Values Report: a clear and simple guide that illustrates the values that resonate most across the collective, painting an authentic picture of what the organization stands for at its grassroots level.

This approach has transformative implications. For one, it acknowledges that as teams evolve and company compositions change, so the values might as well. A company's values are therefore not set in stone; they breathe and grow with the collective input of its members. Furthermore, this co-creative process fosters trust and buy-in. Employees aren't just passive recipients of top-down values; they are active contributors, shaping the future of their organization.

But this isn't to say that a company must adopt every value that emerges from this group report. Organizations can blend these collective values with strategic ones, crafting a set of values that is both authentic and aspirational while also guiding the company towards a desired future.

A case in point is my experience with a German tech firm. On the surface, we might have expected their values to be rooted strictly in innovation or technical excellence. However, when they completed the discovery process, they uncovered two shared core values—the top two, in fact!—that leaders were oblivious to: Flexibility and Harmony. This was a call to action. Recognizing the importance of these values, the company introduced flexible working arrangements, catering to the diverse needs and lifestyles of their employees. Additionally, they invested in training focused on empathy and non-violent communication, acknowledging the significance of harmony in their workplace.

Co-creating company values isn't just about finding common ground; it's about recognizing the collective, honoring individual inputs, and melding these insights into a cohesive value system that drives both purpose and performance.

My advice for any company looking to create or refresh its values is to aim for a spread of values across the Values Pyramid. Every company needs Belonging, Growth, Impact, and Fulfillment values. When we look at some of the world's leading organizations, we see that this is the case. Consider NVIDIA, where the core values are:

- Innovation (Growth + Impact)
- Speed and agility (Growth)

- Intellectual honesty (Growth)
- Excellence (Impact)
- One team (Belonging)

Or Accenture, which values:

- Client value creation (Impact)
- One global network (Impact)
- Respect for the individual (Belonging)
- Best people (Belonging)
- Integrity (Growth)
- Stewardship (Fulfillment)

One last example is Google:

- Protecting users (Impact)
- Building belonging (Belonging)
- Expanding opportunity (Growth)
- Responding to crises (Impact)
- Advancing sustainability (Fulfillment)

While these are great examples, companies should ideally aim for three or four values, for memorability. I'm curious about the percentage of employees at each of the corporate giants listed above who can recall their company values, never mind use them as decision-making tools.

The Importance of Values Diversity

Picture yourself sitting around a campfire, alone beneath the dark night sky. Occasionally one falls, leaving a trail of sparkles—and perhaps a wish or two—in its wake. Our ancestors stared at those same stars. They fought for our survival, and they are still right here with us, their eyes alight with the wisdom—and values—of ages. They knew something fundamental about survival—it was never a solo act.

Within a tribe, having members who valued different things was not only beneficial but essential. While some individuals with a strong sense of curiosity might venture out, seeking new territories or resources, others who valued belonging would focus on community and social bonds. Those who valued freedom might explore innovative solutions to challenges, while those valuing safety would maintain stability and tradition. This mosaic of values created a balanced ecosystem, ensuring that while some took risks, others provided a safety net. It was this adaptive mix of values within a tribe that helped navigate the unpredictability of prehistoric life, laying the foundation for the diverse value systems we observe in societies today.

Whether in an organization, a sports team, or a family, each individual brings a unique set of values, driven by his or her personal experiences, cultural background, and innate predispositions.

While there are various models and theories that seek to understand these predispositions, Deloitte's Business Chemistry stands out as a particularly insightful tool. Derived from a blend of neuroanthropology and data analytics, Business Chemistry builds on existing psychological theories in a practical, accessible format. The model categorizes individuals into four primary types: Guardians, Integrators, Pioneers, and Drivers. Each type has its distinct behavioral patterns, preferences, and, as we'll explore, underlying values.

1. Guardians & Survival Values: Guardians, with their preference for stability, structure, and loyalty, often find alignment with values rooted in the Survival layer. These values, which encompass fundamental needs and security, resonate with the Guardians' intrinsic desire for consistency and reliability in their home and professional environments.

2. Integrators & Belonging Values: The Integrators' innate focus on relationships, consensus-building, and connecting with others corresponds naturally with values in the Belonging category. Their desire for harmony and fostering a sense of community aligns with values that prioritize social connections and acceptance within a group.

3. Pioneers & Growth Values: Pioneers, characterized by their spontaneity, adaptability, and openness to new experiences, often gravitate toward values found in the Growth layer. These values, which advocate for personal and professional evolution, resonate with the Pioneers' zest for exploration and their propensity to challenge the status quo.

4. Drivers & Impact Values: Drivers, with their analytical, results-driven mindset, prioritize values that are seated in the Impact layer. These values emphasize tangible achievements, influence, and the ability to effect change, mirroring the Drivers' ambition and goal-oriented nature.

What about Fulfillment?

As a universal desire, Fulfillment values transcend any specific behavioral style. These values emerge when individuals, regardless of their dominant style, reach a stage where they derive deep satisfaction and meaning from their endeavors. Every style—be it Guardian, Integrator, Pioneer, or Driver—seeks a sense of purpose and significance in their work, making Fulfillment the all-encompassing aspiration.

So How Can We Work Together Better?

Navigating the maze of behavioral dynamics can be daunting, but a model like Business Chemistry helps us understand who is likely to get along and where problems might arise. Here's the big reveal: look at the table below. Vertically and horizontally adjacent styles tend to collaborate well. Diagonal opposites don't always attract. In fact, some of the most tense and toxic interactions I've ever witnessed have been between diagonally opposing styles.

Pioneer

- Innovation
- Creativity
- Openness

Integrator

- Harmony
- Inclusivity
- Connectivity

Driver

- Results
- Directness
- Achievement

Guardian

- Stability
- Tradition
- Reliability

Guardians, anchored by survival values, prioritize stability, reliability, and tradition, excelling in situations requiring consistency and precision. To collaborate effectively with Pioneers, Guardians must value the fresh perspectives Pioneers bring, recognizing that innovation often stems from disruption. Conversely, Pioneers, driven by growth values, are the adventurers who push boundaries and introduce novel ideas. They must value the structure Guardians provide, understanding that groundbreaking ideas need a solid foundation for successful execution. By practicing patience and openness, both groups can appreciate each other's strengths: Pioneers can respect the need for structure, and Guardians can embrace creativity, acknowledging that progress often requires a leap of faith.

Integrators, with values rooted in belonging, emphasize harmony, inclusiveness, and relationship-building; they act as connectors, bridging divides and knitting teams together. Meanwhile, Drivers, with their laser focus on results, thrive on efficiency and achievement. Their straightforward approach can sometimes clash with Integrators' need for harmony. For Integrators to gel with their opposites, the

Drivers, they must strive to understand that a Driver's directness is typically a reflection of their goal-oriented nature, not a dismissal of others' feelings. Conversely, Drivers, fueled by impact values, should cherish the Integrator's ability to foster a positive team environment, realizing that a harmonious atmosphere often leads to increased productivity and satisfaction. By recognizing the Integrators' role in maintaining team cohesion, Drivers can navigate disagreements more smoothly. Integrators can also benefit from understanding the Drivers' need for clear, concise communication, making collaborations more efficient.

You can use a model like this for work, sports, school or even at home. I have helped many organizations gain clarity and increase team performance through deep-dive workshops on this specific topic. By understanding behavioral styles, preferences, and their underlying values, we open up the potential for increased appreciation, cohesion and fulfillment. This should be the priority of every leader. And we are all leaders.

THE VALUE OF NATURE STEWARDSHIP

Nature, with its vast resources, landscapes, and ecosystems, offers us an incredible gift. To be stewards of such treasures is not just an honor but a profound responsibility.

The benefits of nature stewardship are manifold. On an individual level, it fosters a sense of connection and respect towards the environment. This bond translates to mental and physical well-being, as spending time in natural environments has been proven to reduce stress, boost mood, and promote overall health. Furthermore, people who actively participate in stewardship activities, from planting trees to cleaning local waterways, often report a sense of increased purpose and fulfillment.

Collectively, the perks of nature stewardship translate to healthier ecosystems, which in turn support stronger communities. Clean air and water, fertile soil, and biodiversity are essential for our food systems, economies, and overall societal health. Beyond these tangible benefits, stewardship fosters a collective conscience, a shared value around which communities can rally, recognizing the interdependence of all life.

Instead of narrowing our focus to singular environmental issues, such as climate change or species conservation, we ought to expand our vision. By embracing the stewardship of nature as a holistic principle, we can all engage in proactive measures, seeking ways to contribute positively to the environment. Stewardship is not merely about conserving or reacting to crises, but also about forging a sustainable bond with the Earth, understanding its rhythms, and ensuring its vitality.

The "Seven Generations" concept, rooted in Indigenous wisdom, beautifully encapsulates this. It implores us to think ahead, making decisions today that will benefit seven generations into the future. This forward-looking philosophy underpins the essence of nature stewardship—taking care not only for ourselves but for countless generations to come.

On a planet where technology and urbanization continually redefine our relationship with the natural world, embedding nature stewardship into our values is paramount. It is not just about preserving the environment but about crafting a legacy of care, respect, and foresight, ensuring that the wonders of our world are cherished and sustained for millennia to come.

CONCLUSION

A S WE REACH the end of this journey, I would like to thank someone whose values prevented what could have been a bloody civil war. I might not be here today without him. Thank you, Madiba—Nelson Mandela—for staying true to your values of equality, justice, and peace despite unimaginable adversity. Your commitment to the principles of Ubuntu, the belief in a universal bond of sharing that connects all humanity, has inspired countless people around the world.

Mandela's life reminds us that our values are the light that guides us through the darkest of life's challenges; they are the stars by which we chart our path in a world that can be overwhelming at best and terrifying at worst.

In the spirit of Mandela, remember that the power to transform the world around us begins within. If you want to change your external world, change your inner world.

Whenever you stand at the crossroads of decision, let there be two guiding questions to illuminate your path:

- "Will I regret this action (or my silence, for inaction is a choice in itself)?"
- "Will this bring me fulfillment?"

Regret lingers like the echo of words never spoken and paths left untrodden, a specter of "what-ifs" that persists well beyond the crossroads of decision.

Fulfillment, on the other hand, is like the setting sun. First a blinding orb, it mellows as it dips toward the horizon, its form expanding, its contours crisply defined against the twilight sky. In the golden glow of a values-aligned life, fulfillment emerges: a profound realization that the journey was worthwhile. Each step mattered, the dots connected, the ripples of your actions gave others the momentum they needed for their own journeys.

In the story of your life, be the author of chapters filled with boldness and heartfelt decisions. Balance this with rest, reflection, and gratitude. You only have one chance, so gather some friends and mentors, embrace your trials, confront the dragon—whatever that may be—and come home to tell the story. It matters more than you realize.

This is your time.

This is your story.

* * *

As I reach the top of Mount Maunganui in New Zealand, beads of sweat roll down my face. Crimson rays from the sun, our home star—a fission reactor floating in space—caress my skin. I close my eyes for a moment.

I am here now.

I open my eyes and see waves breaking against rocks far below. Swells crisscross towards the harbor. Birds wheel and settle into the cliff face. I touch a courageous plant that grows from a crack in the warm stone. Moments like these bring fulfillment. The journey has been worthwhile.

ACKNOWLEDGMENTS

THANK YOU FOR joining me on this voyage through the science and practice of values. I appreciate your time and energy immensely. If you enjoyed this book and have a few moments, please write a review and post it on Amazon, Goodreads, or wherever you purchased it.

To connect with me, please visit bradleyhook.com, search for "Bradley Hook" on LinkedIn, or follow @bradhook on Instagram. I would be delighted to speak at your next event or share your story on my show, the Brad Hook Podcast.

For further resources, tools, and articles, please visit startwithvalues.com. You'll meet a tribe of like-minded people who would love to connect with you.

If you are interested in the topic of resilience or would like to build a resilient team, I'd be delighted to support you through my work at Resilience Institute Global. We have a passionate values-based team and cutting-edge assessment technology that supports organizations worldwide with game-changing insights and training experiences. Visit resiliencei.com and mention that you read my book to be connected with me.

If you want to use the Start With Values methodology in your company or coaching practice, get certified at startwithvalues.com/values-course.

Thank you once again, and I look forward to staying connected.

ABOUT THE AUTHOR

BRADLEY HOOK IS a writer, speaker and entrepreneur with a focus on human resilience and well-being, advising top-tier organizations worldwide. He is an active partner at The Resilience Institute and has recently started The Values Institute, a personal initiative that aspires to be the world's premier repository on the subject of human core values. Currently living in Mount Maunganui, New Zealand, Brad has traveled extensively around the world. His expertise in intertwining technology, wellbeing, and high performance has made him a sought-after voice.

RESOURCES

The following resources will help you on your journey. Find out more about Brad Hook on bradleyhook.com.

CONNECT WITH BRAD HOOK

Brad Hook Podcast

bradleyhook.com/podcast

Discover the Brad Hook Podcast: a place for the curious. Each episode offers deep dives with diverse guests—from academics demystifying theories to athletes discussing grit, authors revealing their thought processes, or storytellers enchanting with tales. It's a fusion of backgrounds and ideas, aiming to provide listeners with a kaleidoscope of inspiration, knowledge, and passion.

Search "Brad Hook Podcast" in Spotify, Apple Podcasts, and Amazon Music.

Brad's Socials

YouTube: youtube.com/@thebradhook

Instagram: instagram.com/bradhook

LinkedIn: linkedin.com/in/bradleyhook

Other Writing

Newsletter: bradleyhook.com/news

Articles: bradleyhook.com/blog

Books: bradleyhook.com/books

Brad on Entrepreneur Magazine: entrepreneur.com/author/
bradley-hook

Waves of Freedom Documentary

bradleyhook.com/documentary

Surfd.com

PERSONAL VALUES

Discover and align your values with the comprehensive resource library available on startwithvalues.com. Download the Values App at startwithvalues.com/values-app.

THE VALUES COURSE

startwithvalues.com/values-course

Would you like to add the latest tools to your coaching practice? Do you want to champion values within your organization? Are you a leader wanting to upgrade your company culture? Want to create a values-based family or community? Looking for proven ways to reduce your own stress and increase fulfillment?

Sign up for the Values Course and elevate your practice with this guided learning experience.

Articles about values: startwithvalues.com/articles

Books about values: startwithvalues.com/
books-about-core-values

Join the values newsletter: startwithvalues.com/news

Values-based decision-making: startwithvalues.com/decisions

Values meditation: startwithvalues.com/meditation

WORKPLACE VALUES

If you're looking to refresh your company values—or bring them to life with research-based tools—then visit startwithvalues.com.

Workplace Values: startwithvalues.com/values-training

Book a keynote presentation: geniya@startwithvalues.com

Articles about values at work: startwithvalues.com/category/workplace

BUILD RESILIENCE

resiliencei.com/resilience-assessment

Brad Hook is a partner at Resilience Institute Global, a B Corp that is committed to helping organizations achieve performance with care. Brad and the team at Resilience Institute support many of the world's most influential organizations with measurement and training programs. Find out more at resiliencei.com.

Discover how resilient you are: Discover the assessment that is changing how leaders support their teams. Featuring 50 factors that underpin physical, emotional, mental and social fitness, it takes the guesswork out of employee well-being, performance and engagement.

The Resilience Assessment is a scientifically-validated, peer-reviewed toolkit, developed over two decades to deliver unique insights about the human experience at work.

Book a resilience workshop: brad.hook@resiliencei.com

THE RESILIENCE PODCAST

resiliencei.com/podcast

A podcast by the Resilience Institute, hosted by Brad Hook. Dedicated to resilience insights, interviews and practical tips. Search "Resilience Podcast" in Spotify, Apple Podcasts, and Amazon Music.

RESILIENCE MASTERY: 11 KEYS TO UPGRADE HUMAN PERFORMANCE

Resilience Mastery shares the top 11 skills and behaviours shared by individuals who demonstrate exceptionally high resilience. Internationally recognised author, speaker and technologist, Bradley Hook, explores each of these keys in a quest to upgrade human performance and improve our experience of life.

Featuring success stories, anecdotes and practical worksheets the book will help you:

- Improve your focus
- Discover and align with your purpose
- Be more fulfilled
- Develop an optimistic mindset
- Cultivate a lifestyle that supports vitality
- Stay present and calm
- Act decisively
- Bounce through adversity—quickly
- Be more assertive
- Secure quality sleep
- Discover and align with core values

Visit: amzn.to/4e22rvj, or search "Resilience Mastery" in your preferred book store.